Sarah Daniel

AIR FRYER QUICK & EASY
2 cookbooks in 1

EVERYDAY QUICK & EASY RECIPES FOR AIR FRYER LOVERS

Kensington Recipe Press

© 2021 Kensington Recipe Press - All rights reserved.

Photography Humbert Castillo
Graphic design Yuka Okuma
Editorial coordination Lizzie Martin

First edition March 2021

The following book is reproduced below to provide information that is as accurate and reliable as possible. Regardless, purchasing this book can be seen as consent because both the publisher and the author of this book are in no way experts on the topics discussed within. Any recommendations or suggestions that are made herein are for entertainment purposes only. Professionals should be consulted as needed before undertaking any of the actions endorsed herein. This declaration is deemed fair and valid by both the American Bar Association and the Committee of Publishers Association and is legally binding throughout the United States. Furthermore, the transmission, duplication, or reproduction of any of the following work, including specific information, will be considered an illegal act irrespective of if it is done electronically or in print. This extends to creating a secondary or tertiary copy of the work or a recorded document and can only express written consent from the publisher. All additional rights reserved. The information in the following pages is broadly considered a truthful and accurate account of facts. As such, any inattention, use, or misuse of the information in question by the reader will render any resulting actions solely under their purview. There are no scenarios in which the publisher or the original author of this work can be in any fashion deemed liable for any hardship or damages that may befall them after undertaking the information described herein. Additionally, the following pages' information is intended only for informational purposes and should thus be thought of as universal. As befitting its nature, it is presented without assurance regarding its prolonged validity or interim quality. Trademarks that are mentioned are done without written consent and can in no way be considered an endorsement from the trademark holder.

Introduction

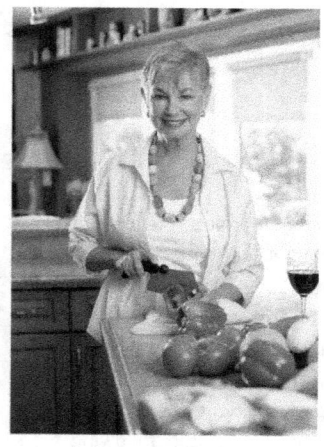

Sarah Daniel is a passionate cookbook writer with over two decades of professional culinary expertise. Known for her culinary skills and high standard, she has combined her classic recipes tailored to use with the modern cooking appliance in her new cookbook series "The Complete Air Fryer Cookbook" for Kensington Recipe Press. She loves to employ innovations in cooking by keeping the traditional elements and richness.

We can always find the art of simplicity in her recipes, making her a step ahead of many innovative cooking methods. All of her books include self-tested recipes, and the pleasure of sharing exciting experiments is evident in most of her recipe works.

Popularly known as a "recipe development whiz" among her circle, she contributes recipes to several reputed magazines. She helps you discover something new and impressive. Beyond her books, she maintains a strong influence among her friends and family as an enthusiast of healthy eating and living.

Having spent considerable time writing the series "The Complete Air Fryer Cookbook", Sarah has carefully penned her research with super versatile meal ideas without compromising quality and nutritional values. Her approach to modern food tech is mind-blowing. This Cookbook Series is a pioneering endeavor blended with modern cooking with traditional values by focusing on healthy, balanced food. It is a reference series for people who love having healthy food.

Table of Content

INTRODUCTION — 8

QUICK & EASY RECIPES — 9

- Tuna Sandwiches — 11
- Eggs and Broccoli Brekky — 12
- Creamy Eggs with Broccoli — 14
- Stuffed Mushrooms — 16
- Artichokes and Tarragon Sauce — 18
- Lemony Artichokes — 19
- Prawn Momos — 20
- Prawn Samosa — 21
- Cheesy Cauliflower Tots — 23
- Crispy Brussels Sprouts — 25
- Buffalo Cauliflower — 27
- Cilantro Lime Roasted Cauliflower — 28
- Coconut Flour Cheesy Garlic Biscuits — 29
- Avocado Impanato — 31
- Potato Spread — 32
- Banana Snack — 34
- Mexican Apple Snack — 35
- Shrimp Muffins — 36
- Zucchini Cakes — 37
- Cauliflower Bars — 38
- Pesto Crackers — 40
- Pumpkin Muffins — 41
- Zucchini Chips — 43
- Honey Party Wings — 44
- Salmon Party Patties — 45
- Banana Chips — 46
- Spring Rolls — 48
- Crispy Radish Chips — 49
- Crab Sticks — 50
- Air Fried Dill Pickles — 52
- Chickpeas Snack — 53
- Bread Sticks — 54
- Crispy Shrimp — 56
- Cajun Shrimp Appetizer — 58
- Shrimp and Chestnut Rolls — 59
- Herbed Tomatoes Appetizer — 61
- Olives Balls — 62

JALAPENO BALLS	64
WRAPPED SHRIMP	66
BROCCOLI PATTIES	67
DIFFERENT STUFFED PEPPERS	68
CHEESY ZUCCHINI SNACK	69
SPINACH BALLS	71
MUSHROOMS APPETIZER	72
CHEESE STICKS	74
SWEET BACON SNACK	76
PORK BURGER CUTLETS	78
LAMB FRIES	79
BARBECUE PORK CLUB SANDWICH	81
PORK BURGER CUTLETS	83
TASTY KALE AND CELERY CRACKERS	84
TUNA CAKES	85
TOASTED SEASONED NUTS	87
NACHO COATED PRAWNS	89
CHEESY MUSTARD AND HAM ROUNDS	90
GRILLED CHEESE DELIGHT	91
ROTI PRATA MINI SAUSAGE ROLLS	92
FILO COVERED APPLE PIE	94
PUFF PASTRY BANANA ROLLS	96
CRUNCHY SWEET POTATO STICKS	97
SPRING ROLLS	98
SYRUPY BUTTERED FIGS WITH MASCARPONE	99
CORN TORTILLA CHIPS	101
AIR FRIED BANANA CHIPS	102
ROSEMARY CHIPS	103
AIR FRIED CRAB STICKS	105
BREAD ROLLS WITH CRISP POTATO STUFFING	106
FETA AND ONION BELL PEPPER ROLLS	108
SPICY COCONUT COATED SHRIMP	110
CRISPY FRENCH FRIES	112
BACON-WRAPPED SHRIMP	113
SAGE AND ONION STUFFING BALLS AIR-FRYER	114
CHENJEHN	116
JUICY KEBAB	118
BANANA ROLLS	120
MILANESE OF EGGPLANT	122
URUGUAYAN FRIED CAKES	124
DELICIOUS MALANGA	125
ARTICHOKE CROQUETTES	126
CARAMELIZED BANANAS	127
BANANA PIE	129

Fried Vegan Milk	130
Celery Fritters	132
Vegan Donuts	134
Andes Cakes	135
Apple Fritters	136
Cinammon Apples	137
Fried Tofu	139
Vegan French Toast with Oregano	140
Vegan Chips	141
Vegetarian Pizza	143

Introduction

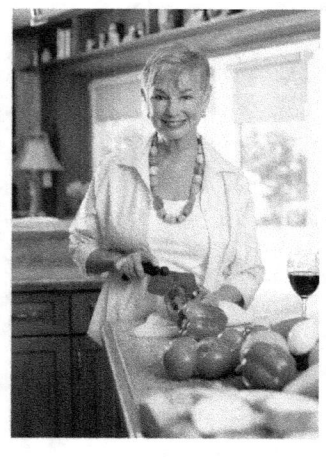

Gale Green is a passionate cookbook writer with over two decades of professional culinary expertise. Known for her culinary skills and high standard, she has combined her classic recipes tailored to use with the modern cooking appliance in her new cookbook series "The Complete Air Fryer Cookbook" for Kendrick Knowles Publishing House. She loves to employ innovations in cooking by keeping the traditional elements and richness.

We can always find the art of simplicity in her recipes, making her a step ahead of many innovative cooking methods. All of her books include self-tested recipes, and the pleasure of sharing exciting experiments is evident in most of her recipe works.

Popularly known as a "recipe development whiz" among her circle, she contributes recipes to several reputed magazines. She helps you discover something new and impressive. Beyond her books, she maintains a strong influence among her friends and family as an enthusiast of healthy eating and living.

Having spent considerable time writing the series "The Complete Air Fryer Cookbook" she has carefully penned her research with super versatile meal ideas without compromising quality and nutritional values. Her approach to modern food tech is mind-blowing.
This Cookbook Series is a pioneering endeavor blended with modern cooking with traditional values by focusing on healthy, balanced food. It is a reference series for people who love having healthy food.

Quick & Easy Recipes

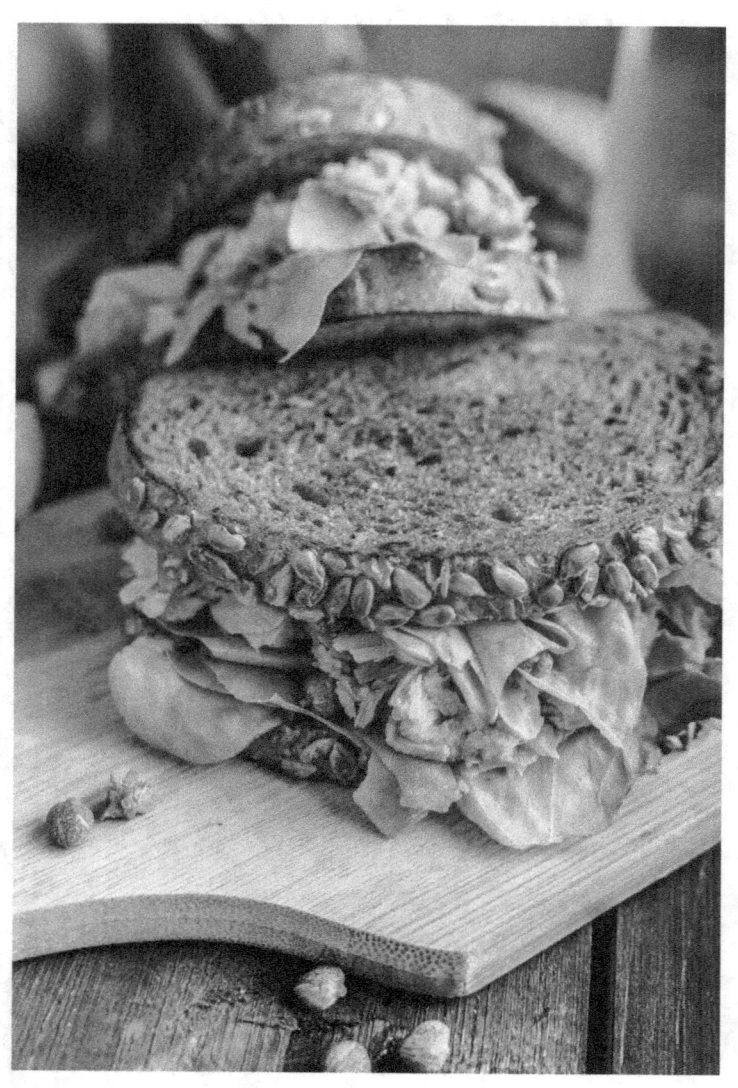

Tuna Sandwiches

Ready in about 15 min | Servings 4 | Easy

Ingredients:

- 16 ounces of canned tuna, drained
- ¼ cup of mayonnaise
- 2 tablespoons of mustard
- 1 tablespoon of lemon juice
- 2 green onions, chopped
- 3 English muffins, halved
- 3 tablespoons of butter
- 6 provolone of cheese

Directions:

1. In a bowl, mix tuna with mayo, lemon juice, mustard, and green onions and stir.
2. Grease muffin halves with the butter, place them in preheated Air Fryer, and bake them at 350° F for 4 minutes.
3. Spread tuna mix on muffin halves, top each with provolone cheese, returns and wishes to Air Fryer and cook them for 4 minutes, divide among plates and serve for breakfast right away.
4. When the timer reaches 0, then press the cancel button

Enjoy!

Eggs and Broccoli Brekky

Ready About in: 20 min| Serves 3|

Ingredients

- ½ cup milk
- ½ cup shredded Cheddar cheese
- 1 cup broccoli, cut into little bits or riced
- 1 cup cauliflower, riced
- 1 teaspoons salt
- 1/2 teaspoon ground black pepper
- 1/2-pound hot pork sausage, diced
- 3 large eggs

Direction:

1. Lightly grease baking pan of Air Fryer with cooking spray. And cook pork sausage for 5 minutes at 360° F.

2. Remove basket and toss the mixture a bit. Stir in riced cauliflower and broccoli. Cook for another 5 minutes.

3. Meanwhile, whisk well eggs, salt, pepper, and milk. Stir in cheese.

4. Remove basket and pour in egg mixture.

5. Cook for another 10 minutes.

6. Serve and enjoy.

Creamy Eggs with Broccoli

Ready about in 20 min| Serves 2| Easy

Ingredients

- 3 Eggs
- 2 tablespoons Cream
- 2 tablespoons Parmesan Cheese grated or cheddar cheese
- Salt to taste
- Black Pepper to taste
- 1/2 cup Broccoli small florets
- 1/2 cup Bell Pepper cut into small pieces

Direction:

1. Lightly grease baking pan of Air Fryer with cooking spray. Spread broccoli florets and bell pepper on bottom and for 7 minutes, cook on 360° F.
2. In a bowl whisk eggs. Stir in cream. Season with pepper and salt.
3. Remove basket and toss the mixture a bit. Pour egg mixture over.
4. Cook for another 10 minutes.
5. Sprinkle cheese and let it rest for 3 minutes.
6. Serve and enjoy.

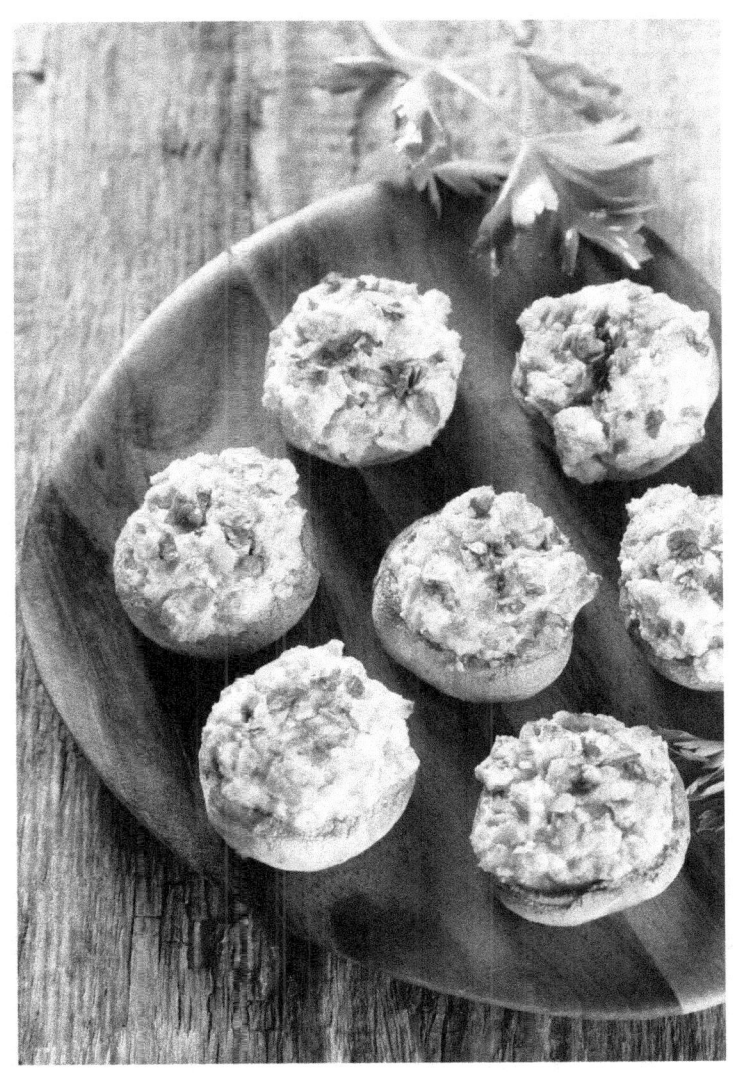

Stuffed Mushrooms

Ready in about 30 min | Servings 4 | Normal

Ingredients:

- 4 big Portobello mushroom caps
- 1 tablespoon of olive oil
- ¼ cup of ricotta cheese
- 5 tablespoons of parmesan, grated
- 1 cup of spinach, torn
- 1/3 cup of bread crumbs
- ¼ teaspoon of rosemary, chopped

Directions:

1. Rub mushrooms caps with the oil, place them in your Air Fryer's basket and cook them at 350° F for 2 minutes.

2. Meanwhile, in a bowl, mix half of the parmesan with ricotta, spinach, rosemary, and bread crumbs and stir well.

3. Stuff mushrooms with this mix, sprinkle the rest of the parmesan on top, place them in your Air Fryer's basket again and cook at 350° F for 10 minutes.

4. Divide them between plates and serve with a side salad for lunch. Enjoy!

Artichokes and Tarragon Sauce

Ready in about 28 min | Servings 4 | Easy

Ingredients:

- 4 artichokes, trimmed
- 2 tablespoons of tarragon, chopped
- 2 tablespoons of chicken stock
- Lemon zest from 2 lemons, grated
- 2 tablespoons of lemon juice
- 1 celery stalk, chopped
- ½ cup of olive oil
- Salt to the taste

Directions:

1. In your food processor, mix tarragon, chicken stock, lemon zest, lemon juice, celery, salt, and olive oil and pulse very well.
2. In a bowl, mix artichokes with tarragon and lemon sauce, toss well, transfer them to your Air Fryer's basket and cook at 380° F for 18 minutes.
3. Divide artichokes between plates, drizzle the rest of the sauce all over and serve as a side dish.

Enjoy!

Lemony Artichokes

Ready in about 25 min | Servings 4 | Easy

Ingredients:

- 2 medium artichokes, trimmed and halved
- Cooking spray
- 2 tablespoons of lemon juice
- Salt and black pepper to the taste

Directions:

1. Grease your Air Fryer with cooking spray, add artichokes, drizzle lemon juice and sprinkle salt and black pepper and cook them at 380° F for 15 minutes.

2. Select bake mode the set the temperature to

3. Divide them between plates and serve as a side dish.

Enjoy!

Prawn Momos

Ready in about 30 min | Servings 2 | Normal

Ingredients:

For the dough:

- 1 ½ cup all-purpose flour
- ½ tsp. salt
- 5 tbsp. water

For the filling:

- 2 cups of minced prawn
- 2 tbsp. of oil
- 2 tsp. of ginger-garlic paste
- 2 tsp. of soy sauce
- 2 tsp. of vinegar

Directions:

1. Knead and cover the dough with plastic wrap, then set aside. Prepare the filling ingredients, and try to make sure the prawn is properly coated with the sauce.

2. Print out the dough, then cut it into a rectangle. Place the center filling. Fold the dough now to protect the filling, then pinch the corners.

3. Preheat up the Air Fryer 5 minutes at 200° F. Drop the wontons into and close the fry basket. Let them cook for another 20 minutes, at the same time. Recommended sides contain chili or ketchup sauce.

Prawn Samosa

Ready in about 25 min | Servings 2 | Normal

Ingredients:

For wrappers:

- 2 tablespoons of unsalted butter
- 1 ½ cup of all-purpose flour
- A pinch of salt to taste
- Add as much water as required to make the dough stiff and firm

For filling:

- 1 lb. of prawn
- ¼ cup of boiled peas
- 1 tsp. of powdered ginger
- 1 or 2 green chilies that are finely chopped or mashed
- ½ teaspoon of cumin
- 1 teaspoon of coarsely crushed coriander
- 1 dry red chili broken into pieces
- A small amount of salt (to the taste)
- ½ teaspoon of dried mango powder
- ½ teaspoon of red chili powder.
- 1-2 teaspoon of coriander.

Directions:

1. First, you would have to make the exterior shell. Put the flour, butter, and enough water in a large bowl to knead it into a hard dough.

2. Switch everything to a jar and quit for five minutes to relax. Place a saucepan over medium flame and add the oil. Whisk the mustard seeds and add the coriander seeds and the diced dried red chilies until roasted. Place all the dry ingredients into the filling and combine properly.

3. Put them in water, so the ingredients begin to boil. Shape the dough into little balls and roll them out. Break the rolled-out dough in half and add some water on the sides to help shape the halves into a triangle.

4. Attach the cone lining, and remove the samosa—Preheat the Air Fryer at 300° F for around 5-6 minutes. In the fry basket, put all the samosas and close the basket properly.

5. Hold the Air Fryer for another 20 to 25 minutes, at 200° F. Open the basket at the halfway mark, and turn over the samosas for standard preparation. After this, fry for around 10 minutes at 250° F to give them the perfect golden-brown hue. Serve wet. Recommended sides are chutney with tamarind or mint.

Cheesy Cauliflower Tots

Ready in about 30 min | Servings 6 | Easy

Ingredients:

- 1 large head of cauliflower
- 1 cup of shredded mozzarella cheese
- 1/2 cup of grated Parmesan cheese
- 1 large egg
- 1/4 teaspoon of garlic powder
- 1/4 teaspoon of dried parsley
- 1/8 teaspoon of onion powder

Directions:

1. Fill a big pot with 2 cups of water on the stovetop, and insert a steamer in the oven. Put to boil bath. Break the cauliflower into flower and placed on a steamer box—cover pot and lid.

2. Let steam the cauliflower for 7 minutes until it is tender. Put in the cheese cloth or clean kitchen towel from the steamer basket and let it cool. Push on the sink to eliminate as much extra humidity as possible. If not all of the moisture is removed, the mixture will be too soft to form into tots. Mash down to a smooth consistency with a blade.

3. In a large mixing bowl, put the cauliflower and add the mozzarella, parmesan, egg, garlic powder, parsley, and onion powder. Remove until well combined. The blend should be smooth but easy to mold.

4. Take 2 tablespoons of the mixture and roll the mixture into a tot form. Repeat with mixture leftover. Put the basket into the Air Fryer.

5. Select bake mode the set the temperature to 320° F and adjust the timer for 12 minutes.

6. Turn the tots halfway through the period of cooking. Cauliflower tots should be golden when fully cooked. Serve warm.

Crispy Brussels sprouts

Ready in about 15 min | Servings 4 | Easy

Ingredients:

- 1-pound of Brussels sprouts
- 1 tablespoon of coconut oil
- 1 tablespoon of un salted butter, melted

Directions:

1. Extract all sprouts of loose leaves from Brussels and cut in half each.
2. Spray with coconut oil and put it in the basket of the Air Fryer.
3. Select bake mode the set the temperature to 400° F and change the timer for 10 minutes. You may want to stir gently halfway through the cooking time, depending on how they start browning.
4. When the timer reaches 0, then press the cancel button
5. They should be tender with darker caramelized spots when fully baked. Drizzle with melted butter and cut from the fryer bowl. Serve forthwith.

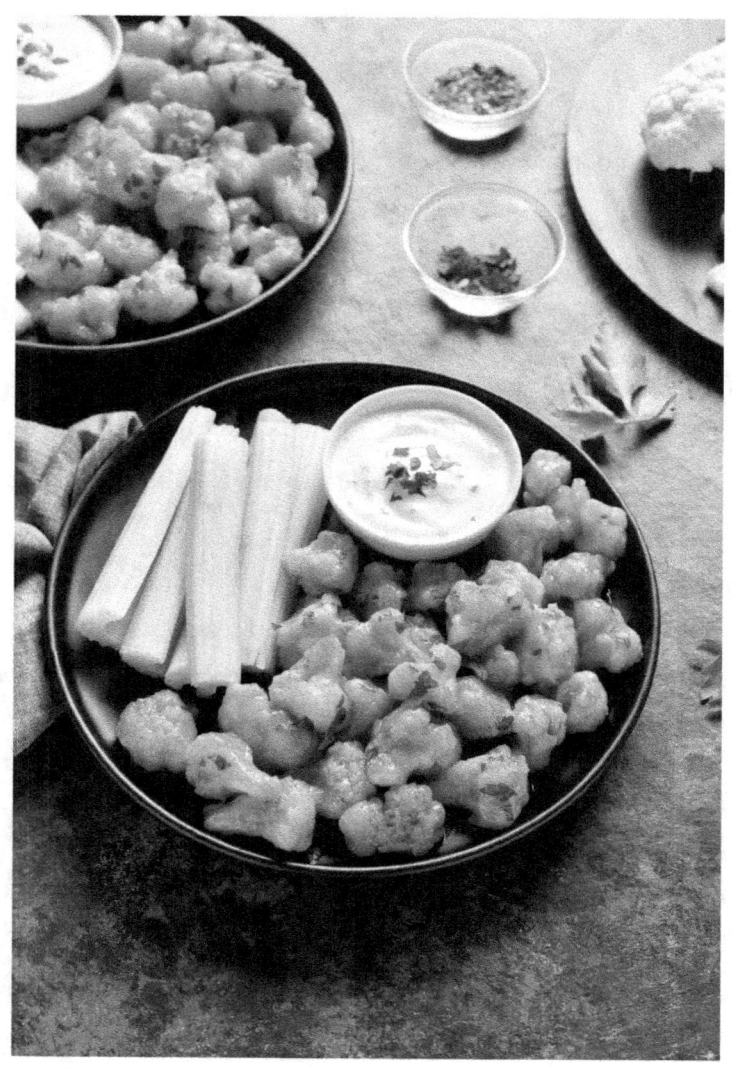

Buffalo Cauliflower

Ready in about 10 min | Servings 4 | Easy

Ingredients:

- 4 cups of cauliflower florets
- 2 tablespoons of salted butter, melted
- 1/2 (1-ounce) dry ranch seasoning packet
- 1/4 cup of buffalo sauce

Directions:

1. In a large bowl, toss cauliflower with butter and dry ranch. Place into the Air Fryer basket.
2. Adjust the temperature to 400° F and set the timer for 5 minutes.
3. Shake the basket 2 or 3 times during cooking. When tender, remove the cauliflower from the fryer basket and toss in buffalo sauce. Serve warm.

Cilantro Lime Roasted Cauliflower

Ready in about 17 min | Servings 4 | Easy

Ingredients:

- 2 cups of chopped cauliflower florets
- 2 tablespoons of coconut oil, melted
- 2teaspoons of chili powder
- 1/2 teaspoon of garlic powder
- 1 medium lime
- 2 tablespoons of chopped cilantro

Directions:

1. Mix the cauliflower in a wide bowl of coconut oil. Sprinkle with ground chili and garlic. Place seasoned cauliflower in the basket for Air Fryer.

2. Select bake mode the set the temperature to 350° F and change the timer for 7 minutes.

3. The cauliflower gets moist and begins to become golden on the sides. Set in a bowl to eat.

4. Cut the lime into quarters and pour cauliflower juice over it. Garnish with coriander.

Enjoy!

Coconut Flour Cheesy Garlic Biscuits

Ready in about 22 min | Servings 4 | Easy

Ingredients:

- 1/3 cup of coconut flour
- 1/2 teaspoon of baking powder
- 1/2 teaspoon of garlic powder
- 1 large egg
- 1/4 cup of unsalted butter, melted and divided
- 1/2 cup of shredded sharp Cheddar cheese
- 1 scallion, sliced

Directions:

1. Mix the coconut flour, baking powder, and garlic powder in a big dish.

2. Add the egg, half the melting butter, the cheddar cheese, and the scallions. Pour the mixture into a 6 " circular baking pan. Put it inside the frame of the Air Fryer.

3. Select bake mode the set the temperature to 320° F and change the timer for 12 minutes.

4. When the timer reaches 0, then press the cancel button

5. Remove from the pan to eat, and allow to cool entirely. Slice into four pieces and pour over each remaining butter.

Enjoy!

Avocado Impanato

Ready in about 22 min | Servings 4 | Easy

Ingredients:

- 2 medium avocados
- ½ teaspoon ground black pepper
- ½ cup panko bread crumbs
- 1 teaspoon water
- 1 Egg
- ¼ teaspoon salt

Directions:

1. Mix flour, pepper, and salt together in a shallow bowl. Beat together egg and water in a second shallow bowl. Place panko in a third shallow bowl.

2. Cut out half of each avocado. Break the fuselage. Remove the peel gently.

3. Dredge an avocado slice through the flour, shaking off excess. Dip into egg and allow excess to drop off. Finally press slice into panko so both sides are covered. Set on a plate and repeat with the remaining slices.

4. Select bake mode the set the temperature to 400° F and set the timer for 5 minutes, Turn avocado slices over and cook until golden, about 2 more minutes.

5. When the timer reaches 0, then press the cancel button

6. Serve warm.

Potato Spread

Ready in about 20 min | Servings 10 | Normal

Ingredients:

- 19 ounces of canned garbanzo beans, drained
- 1 cup of sweet potatoes, peeled and chopped
- ¼ cup of tahini
- 2 tablespoons of lemon juice
- 1 tablespoon of olive oil
- 5 garlic cloves, minced
- ½ teaspoon of cumin, ground
- 2 tablespoons of water
- A pinch of salt and white pepper

Directions:

1. Place the potatoes in the basket of your Air Fryer, cook them for 15 minutes at 360° F, cool them down, peel them, position them in the food processor, and pulse well.

2. Apply the paste of sesame, the garlic, the beans, the lemon juice, the cumin, the water, and the oil.

3. Add salt and pepper, run over again, split and serve in cups.

Enjoy!

Banana Snack

Preparation time: 10 min | Cooking time: 5 min |Servings: 8

Ingredients:

- 16 baking cups of crust
- ¼ cup of peanut butter
- ¾ cup of chocolate chips
- 1 banana, peeled and sliced into 16 pieces
- 1 tablespoon of vegetable oil

Directions:

1. Place chocolate chips in a small container, heat up over low heat, swirl until they melt, and turn off.
2. Mix peanut butter and coconut oil in a cup, then shake well.
3. Mix 1 teaspoon of chocolate in a cup, add 1 slice of banana and 1 teaspoon butter mixture on top
4. Repeat with the rest of the cups, put them all in a dish that suits your Air Fryer, cook for 5 minutes at 320° F, move to a freezer, and remain there until eaten as a snack.
Enjoy!

Mexican Apple Snack

Ready in about 25 min | Servings 4 | Normal

Ingredients:

- 3 big apples, cored, peeled, and cubed
- 2 teaspoons of lemon juice
- ¼ cup of pecans, chopped
- ½ cup of dark chocolate chips
- ½ cup of clean caramel sauce

Directions:

1. Mix apples and lemon juice in a cup, mix and switch to a saucepan that suits your Air Fryer.
2. Add chocolate chips, pecans, drizzle the caramel sauce, swirl, stir in the Air Fryer and cock for 5 minutes at 320° F.
3. When the timer reaches 0, then press the cancel button
4. Kindly mix, break into tiny bowls and serve as a snack right away. Enjoy!

Shrimp Muffins

Ready in about 35 min | Servings 6 | Normal

Ingredients:

- 1 spaghetti squash, peeled and halved
- 2 tablespoons of mayonnaise
- 1 cup of mozzarella, shredded
- 8 ounces shrimp, peeled, cooked, and chopped
- 1 and ½ cups of panko
- 1 teaspoon of parsley flakes
- 1 garlic clove, minced
- Salt and black pepper to the taste
- Cooking spray

Directions:

1. Place the squash halves in the Air Fryer, cook for 16 minutes at 350° F, set aside to cool off, and scrape the flesh into a dish.
2. Stir well and apply salt, pepper, parsley flakes, panko, lobster, mayo, and mozzarella.
3. Spray a muffin tray that blends in with the frying spray in your Air Fryer and place squash and shrimp mix in each cup.
4. Stir in the fryer and cook for 10 minutes at 360° F.
5. Placed muffins on a tray and serve as a snack.

Enjoy!

Zucchini Cakes

Ready in about 25 min | Servings 12 | Normal

Ingredients:

- Cooking spray
- ½ cup of dill, chopped
- 1 egg
- ½ cup of whole wheat flour
- Salt and black pepper to the taste
- 1 yellow onion, chopped
- 2 garlic cloves, minced
- 3 zucchinis, grated

Directions:

1. Mix the zucchinis in a bowl with the garlic, onion, flour, salt, pepper, egg, and dill, stir well, form small patties out of this blend, spray them with cooking spray, put them in the basket of your Air Fryer and cook at 370° F per side for 6 minutes.
2. When the timer reaches 0, then press the cancel button
3. Only serve them as an instant snack.

Enjoy!

Cauliflower Bars

Ready in about 35 min | Servings 12 | Normal

Ingredients:

- 1 big cauliflower head, florets separated
- ½ cup of mozzarella, shredded
- ¼ cup of egg whites
- 1 teaspoon of Italian seasoning
- Salt and black pepper to the taste

Directions:

1. Put cauliflower flowers in your food processor, pulse well, scatter them over a lined baking sheet that suits your Air Fryer, add them to the fryer and cook for 10 minutes at 360° F.

2. Move cauliflower to a cup, add salt, pepper, cheese and egg whites, stir well, spread into a rectangular saucepan that suits your fryer, press well, place in the fryer and cook for 15 minutes at 360° F.

3. Break into 12 strips, put on a plate, and serve as a snack.

Enjoy!

Pesto Crackers

Ready in about 25 min | Servings 6 | Normal

Ingredients:

- ½ teaspoon of baking powder
- Salt and black pepper to the taste
- 1 and ¼ cups of flour
- ¼ teaspoon of basil, dried
- 1 garlic clove, minced
- 2 tablespoons of basil pesto
- 3 tablespoons of butter

Directions:

1. Mix the salt, pepper, baking powder, flour, garlic, cayenne, basil, pesto, and butter in a bowl and stir until a dough is obtained.
2. Put this dough on an Air Fryer-fitting lined baking dish, put it in the fryer at 325° F, and bake for 17 minutes.
3. Set aside to cool off, break and eat crackers as a snack.

Pumpkin Muffins

Ready in about 25 min | Servings 18 | Normal

Ingredients:

- ¼ cup of butter
- ¾ cup of pumpkin puree
- 2 tablespoons of flaxseed meal
- ¼ cup of flour
- ½ cup of sugar
- ½ teaspoon of nutmeg, ground
- 1 teaspoon of cinnamon powder
- ½ teaspoon of baking soda
- 1 egg
- ½ teaspoon of baking powder

Directions:

1. Mix butter and pumpkin puree and egg in a cup, then blend properly.
2. Stir well and incorporate flaxseed meal, flour, sugar, baking soda, baking powder, nutmeg, and cinnamon.
3. Place this in a muffin pan that suits your Air Fryer at 350° F in the Fryer, and bake for 15 minutes.
4. Serve frozen muffins as a snack.

Enjoy!

Zucchini Chips

Ready in about 45 min | Servings 6 | Normal

Ingredients:

- 3 zucchinis, thinly sliced
- Salt and black pepper to the taste
- 2 tablespoons of olive oil
- 2 tablespoons of balsamic vinegar

Directions:

1. Mix oil and vinegar, salt and pepper in a cup, then whisk well.

2. Add the zucchini strips, mix well to cover, place in the Air Fryer and cook for 30 minutes at 200° F.

3. When the timer reaches 0, then press the cancel button

4. Serve frozen corvette chips as a snack.

Enjoy!

Honey Party Wings

Ready in about 25 min | Servings 6 | Normal

Ingredients:

- 16 chicken wings, halved
- 2 tablespoons of soy sauce
- 2 tablespoons of honey
- Salt and black pepper to the taste
- 2 tablespoons of lime juice

Directions:

1. Mix the chicken wings in a bowl of soy sauce, sugar, salt, pepper, and lime juice, mix well, and hold for 1 hour in the refrigerator.
2. Switch the chicken wings to the Air Fryer and cook them for 12 minutes at 360° F, slicing them in half.
3. Put them up on a tray and serve as an appetizer.

Enjoy!

Salmon Party Patties

Ready in about 35 min | Servings 4 | Normal

Ingredients:

- 3 big potatoes, boiled, drained, and mashed
- 1 big salmon fillet, skinless, boneless
- 2 tablespoons of parsley, chopped
- 2 tablespoon of dill, chopped
- Salt and black pepper to the taste
- 1 egg
- 2 tablespoons of bread crumbs
- Cooking spray

Directions:

1. Place salmon in your Air Fryer's basket and cook for 10 minutes at 360°F.
2. Transfer salmon to a cutting board, cool it down, flake it, and put it in a bowl.
3. Add mashed potatoes, salt, pepper, dill, parsley, egg, and bread crumbs, stir well, and shape 8 patties out of this mix.
4. Place salmon patties in your Air Fryer's basket, spray them with cooking oil, cook at 360° F for 12 minutes, flipping them halfway, transfer them to a platter and serve as an appetizer.

Enjoy!

Banana Chips

Ready in about 35 min | Servings 4 | Norma

Ingredients:

- 4 bananas, peeled and sliced
- A pinch of salt
- ½ teaspoon of turmeric powder
- ½ teaspoon of chat masala
- 1 teaspoon of olive oil

Directions:

1. In a bowl, mix banana slices with salt, turmeric, chat masala, and oil, toss and leave aside for 10 minutes.
2. Transfer banana slices to your preheated Air Fryer at 360° F and cook them for 15 minutes, flipping them once.
3. When the timer reaches 0, then press the cancel button
4. Serve as a snack.

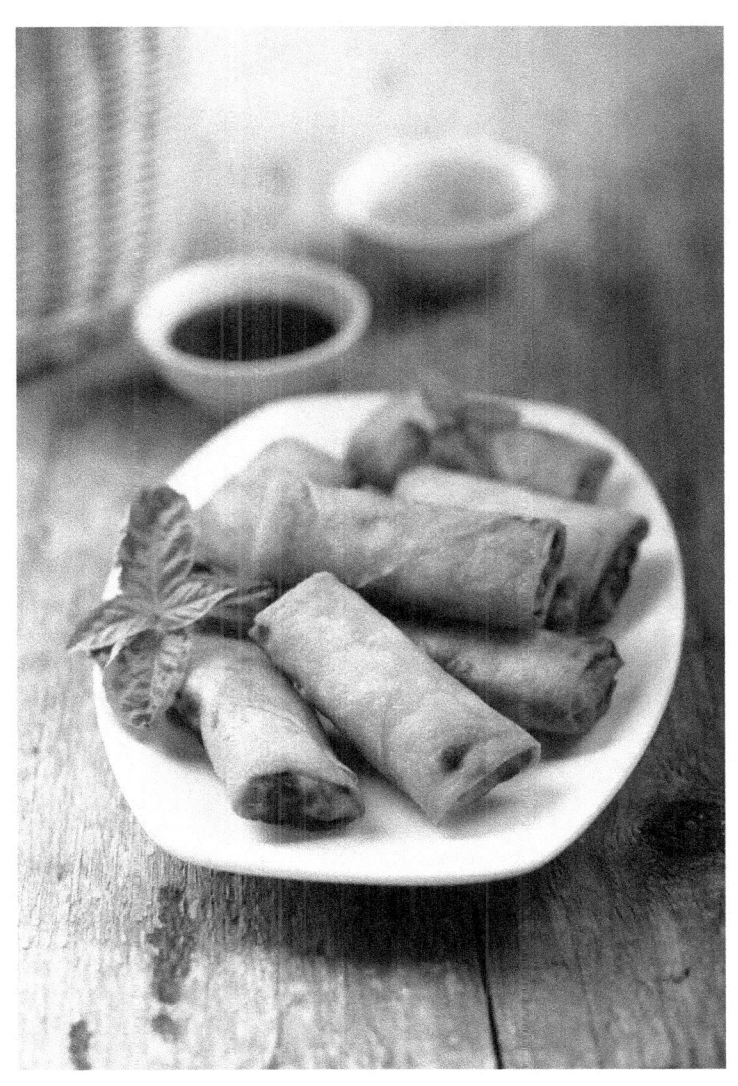

Spring Rolls

Ready in about 35 min | Servings 6 | Normal

Ingredients:

- 2 cups of green cabbage, shredded
- 2 yellow onions, chopped
- 1 carrot, grated
- ½ chili pepper, minced
- 1 tablespoon of ginger, grated
- 3 garlic cloves, minced
- 1 teaspoon of sugar
- Salt and black pepper to the taste
- 1 teaspoon of soy sauce
- 2 tablespoons of olive oil
- 10 spring roll sheets
- 2 tablespoons of water

Directions:

1. Heat a skillet over medium heat with the oil, add cabbage, onions, carrots, chili pepper, ginger, garlic, sugar, salt, pepper, and soy sauce, mix well, cook for 2-3 minutes, heat off and cool off.
2. Break spring roll sheets into squares, divide and roll cabbage mix on top.
3. Mix cornflour with water in a tub, stir well, and use this mix to seal spring rolls.
4. Put spring rolls in the basket of your Air Fryer, and cook them for 10 minutes at 360° F.
5. Flip the rollover and simmer for another 10 minutes.
6. Set aside on a plate and serve as an appetizer.

Crispy Radish Chips

Ready in about 25 min | Servings 4 | Normal

Ingredients:

- Cooking spray
- 15 radishes, sliced
- Salt and black pepper to the taste
- 1 tablespoon of chives, chopped

Directions:

1. Arrange radish slices in your Air Fryer's basket, spray them with cooking oil, season with salt and black pepper to the taste, cook them at 350° F for 10 minutes, flipping them halfway, transfer to bowls.
2. When the timer reaches 0, then press the cancel button
3. serve with chives sprinkled on top.

Crab Sticks

Ready in about 25 min | Servings 4 | Normal

Ingredients:

- 10 crabsticks, halved
- 2 teaspoons of sesame oil
- 2 teaspoons of Cajun seasoning

Directions:

1. Place the crab sticks in a tub, add the sesame oil and the Cajun seasoning, shake, move them to the basket of your Air Fryer and cook for 12 minutes at 350° F. Arrange on a tray.

2. When the timer reaches 0, then press the cancel button

3. serve as an appetizer.

Air Fried Dill Pickles

Ready in about 25 min | Servings 4 | Normal

Ingredients:

- 16 ounces jarred dill pickles, cut into wedges and pat dry
- ½ cup of white flour
- 1 egg
- ¼ cup of milk
- ½ teaspoon of garlic powder
- ½ teaspoon of sweet paprika
- Cooking spray
- ¼ cup of ranch sauce

Directions:

1. In a bowl, combine milk with egg and whisk well.
2. In a second bowl, mix flour with salt, garlic powder, and paprika and stir as well
3. Dip pickles in flour, then in the egg mix and again in flour, and place them in your Air Fryer.
4. Grease them with cooking spray, cook pickle wedges at 400° F for 5 minutes, transfer to a bowl, and serve with ranch sauce on the side.
Enjoy!

Chickpeas Snack

Ready in about 25 min | Servings 4 | Normal

Ingredients:

- 15 ounces of canned chickpeas, drained
- ½ teaspoon of cumin, ground
- 1 tablespoon of olive oil
- 1 teaspoon of smoked paprika
- Salt and black pepper to the taste

Directions:

1. Mix the chickpeas with oil, cumin, paprika, salt, and pepper in a dish, mix to cover, put them in the basket of your Air Fryer and cook for 10 minutes at 390° F.
2. When the timer reaches 0, then press the cancel button
3. Serve as a snack and break into bowls.

Enjoy!

Bread Sticks

Ready in about 20 min | Servings 2 | Norma

Ingredients:

- 4 bread slices, each cut into 4 sticks
- 2 eggs
- ¼ cup of milk
- 1 teaspoon of cinnamon powder
- 1 tablespoon of honey
- ¼ cup of brown sugar
- A pinch of nutmeg

Directions:

1. In a cup, mix milk, brown sugar, cinnamon, nutmeg, and honey with the eggs and whisk well.
2. In this mix, dip the bread sticks, put them in the basket from your Air Fryer, and cook for 10 minutes at 360° F.
3. Divide sticks of bread into bowls and serve as a snack.

Enjoy!

Crispy Shrimp

Ready in about 15 min | Servings 4 | Normal

Ingredients:

- 12 big shrimp, deveined and peeled
- 2 egg whites
- 1 cup of coconut, shredded
- 1 cup of panko bread crumbs
- 1 cup of white flour
- Salt and black pepper to the taste

Directions:

1. In a bowl, mix panko with coconut and stir.
2. Put flour, salt, and pepper in a second bowl and whisk egg whites in a third one.
3. Dip shrimp in flour, egg whites mix, and coconut, place them all in your Air Fryer's basket, cook at 350° F for 10 minutes, flipping halfway.
4. Arrange on a platter and serve as an appetizer.

Cajun Shrimp Appetizer

Ready in about 15 min | Servings 2 | Normal

Ingredients:

- 20 tiger shrimp, peeled and deveined
- Salt and black pepper to the taste
- ½ teaspoon of old bay seasoning
- 1 tablespoon of olive oil
- ¼ teaspoon of smoked paprika

Directions:

1. Mix shrimp and oil, salt, pepper, old bay seasoning, paprika in a dish, and mix to cover.
2. Place shrimp in the basket of your Air Fryer and cook for 5 minutes at 390° F.
3. Put them up on a tray and act as an appetizer.

Enjoy!

Shrimp and Chestnut Rolls

Ready in about 25 min | Servings 4 | Normal

Ingredients:

- ½ pound of already cooked shrimp, chopped
- 8 ounces of water chestnuts, chopped
- ½ pounds of shiitake mushrooms, chopped
- 2 cups of cabbage, chopped
- 2 tablespoons of olive oil
- 1 garlic clove, minced
- 1 teaspoon of ginger, grated
- 3 scallions, chopped
- Salt and black pepper to the taste
- 1 tablespoon of water
- 1 egg yolk
- 6 spring roll wrappers

Directions:

1. Heat a skillet over medium-high heat with the oil, add cabbage, shrimp, chestnuts, mushrooms, garlic, ginger, salt, and pepper, stir and simmer for 2 minutes.
2. Mix the egg and water in a dish, then combine well.
3. Arrange roll wrappers on a working board, slice shrimp and veggie mix into them, seal edges with egg wash, put them all in the basket of your Air Fryer, cook for 15 minutes at 360° F, move to a plate, and serve as an appetizer.

Herbed Tomatoes Appetizer

Ready in about 30 min | Servings 2 | Normal

Ingredients:

- 2 tomatoes, halved
- Cooking spray
- Salt and black pepper to the taste
- 1 teaspoon of parsley, dried
- 1 teaspoon of basil, dried
- 1 teaspoon of oregano, dried
- 1 teaspoon of rosemary, dried

Directions:

1. Sprinkle tomato halves over them with cooking oil, season them with salt, pepper, parsley, basil, oregano, and rosemary.
2. Place these in the basket of your Air Fryer and cook for 20 minutes at 320° F.
3. Put them up on a tray and act as an appetizer.

Enjoy!

Olives Balls

Ready in about 14 min | Servings 6 | Normal

Ingredients:

- 8 black olives, pitted and minced
- Salt and black pepper to the taste
- 2 tablespoons of sun-dried tomato pesto
- 14 pepperoni slices, chopped
- 4 ounces of cream cheese
- 1 tablespoon of basil, chopped

Directions:

1. Mix the cream cheese with salt, pepper, basil, pepperoni, pesto, and black olives in a cup, stir well, and make small balls out of the mixture.
2. Place them in the basket of your Air Fryer, cook for 4 minutes at 350° F, arrange them on a plate
3. When the timer reaches 0, then press the cancel button
4. Serve as a snack.

Enjoy!

Jalapeno Balls

Ready in about 14 min | Servings 3 | Normal

Ingredients:

- 3 bacon slices, cooked and crumbled
- 3 ounces of cream cheese
- ¼ teaspoon of onion powder
- Salt and black pepper to the taste
- 1 jalapeno pepper, chopped
- ½ teaspoon of parsley, dried
- ¼ teaspoon of garlic powder

Directions:

1. Mix cream cheese and jalapeno paste, onion and garlic powder, parsley, bacon, salt, and pepper in a bowl and mix well.
2. Shape tiny balls out of this mix, put them in the basket of your Air Fryer, cook for 4 minutes at 350° F, place them on a platter
3. When setting a cooking time less than 20 minutes, first set the cooking time to 20 minutes.
Then, turn the time/darkness control knob to the desired cooking time
4. Serve as an appetizer.
Enjoy!

Wrapped Shrimp

Ready in about 18 min | Servings 16 | Normal

Ingredients:

- 2 tablespoons of olive oil
- 10 ounces of already cooked shrimp, peeled and deveined
- 1 tablespoon of mint, chopped
- 1/3 cup of blackberries, ground
- 11 prosciuttos sliced
- 1/3 cup of red wine

Directions:

1. Wrap each shrimp into a slice of prosciutto, drizzle the oil over them, rub well, put 390° F in your preheated Air Fryer and fry them for 8 minutes.

2. In the meantime, fire up a skillet over medium heat with ground blackberries, add mint and juice, mix, simmer for 3 minutes and take off the heat.

3. Place shrimp on a platter, sauce blackberries over them, and serve as an appetizer.

Enjoy!

Broccoli Patties

Ready in about 20 min | Servings 12 | Normal

Ingredients:

- 4 cups of broccoli florets
- 1 and ½ cup of almond flour
- 1 teaspoon of paprika
- Salt and black pepper to the taste
- 2 eggs
- ¼ cup of olive oil
- 2 cups of cheddar cheese, grated
- 1 teaspoon of garlic powder
- ½ teaspoon of apple cider vinegar
- ½ teaspoon of baking soda

Directions:

1. In your food processor, place broccoli florets, add salt and pepper, blend well, and move to a dish.
2. Add the almond flour, cinnamon, pepper, paprika, garlic powder, baking soda, butter, milk, eggs, and vinegar, blend well, and form 12 patties from this mixture.
3. Place them in the basket of your preheated Air Fryer and cook for 10 minutes at 350° F.
4. Place patties on a pan, and act as an appetizer.

Enjoy!

Different Stuffed Peppers

Ready in about 30 min | Servings 6 | Normal

Ingredients:

- 1-pound of mini bell peppers halved
- Salt and black pepper to the taste
- 1 teaspoon of garlic powder
- 1 teaspoon of sweet paprika
- ½ teaspoon of oregano, dried
- ¼ teaspoon of red pepper flakes
- 1-poundof beef meat, ground
- 1 and ½ cups of cheddar cheese, shredded
- 1 tablespoon of chili powder
- 1 teaspoon of cumin, ground
- Sour cream for serving

Directions:

1. In a cup, blend and stir together chili powder with paprika, salt, pepper, cumin, oregano, pepper flakes, and garlic powder.
2. Heat a casserole over medium pressure, add beef, stir and brown for 10 min.
3. Add mixture of chili powder, stir, take off the heat and fill halves of pepper with this mix.
4. Sprinkle the cheese all over, put the peppers in the basket from your Air Fryer, and roast them for 6 minutes at 350° F.
5. Arrange peppers on a tray, then eat them vertically with sour cream. Enjoy!

Cheesy Zucchini Snack

Ready in about 18 min | Servings 4 | Normal

Ingredients:

- 1 cup of mozzarella, shredded
- ¼ cup of tomato sauce
- 1 zucchini, sliced
- Salt and black pepper to the taste
- A pinch of cumin
- Cooking spray

Directions:

1. Arrange the zucchini slices in the basket of your Air Fryer, spray them with cooking oil, scatter the tomato sauce all over, season them with salt, pepper, cumin, sprinkle the mozzarella at the end, and roast them for 8 minutes at 320° F.

2. Put them up on a tray and serve as a snack.

Enjoy!

Spinach Balls

Ready in about 17 min | Servings 30 | Normal

Ingredients:

- 4 tablespoons of butter, melted
- 2 eggs
- 1 cup of flour
- 16 ounces of spinach
- 1/3 cup of feta cheese, crumbled
- ¼ teaspoon of nutmeg, ground
- 1/3 cup of parmesan, grated
- Salt and black pepper to the taste
- 1 tablespoon of onion powder
- 3 tablespoons of whipping cream
- 1 teaspoon of garlic powder

Directions:

1. Mix spinach with butter, milk, pasta, feta cheese, parmesan, nutmeg, whipped cream, salt, pepper, onion, and garlic powder in your blender, mix very well and carry for 10 minutes in the freezer.

2. When setting a cooking time less than 20 minutes, first set the cooking time to 20 minutes.

Then, turn the time/darkness control knob to the desired cooking time

3. Shape 30 spinach balls, put them in the basket of your Air Fryer, and cook for 7 minutes at 300° F.

4. Serve as an appetizer to a crowd.

Enjoy!

Mushrooms Appetizer

Ready in about 20 min | Servings 4 | Normal

Ingredients:

- ¼ cup of mayonnaise
- 1 teaspoon of garlic powder
- 1 small yellow onion, chopped
- 24 ounces of white mushroom caps
- Salt and black pepper to the taste
- 1 teaspoon of curry powder
- 4 ounces of cream cheese, soft
- ¼ cup of sour cream
- ½ cup of Mexican cheese, shredded
- 1 cup of shrimp, cooked, peeled, deveined, and chopped

Directions:

1. Mix mayo to blend and shake well in a bowl with garlic powder, onion, curry powder, cream cheese, sour cream, Mexican cheese, seafood, salt, and pepper.
2. Stuff the mushrooms with this mixture put them in the basket from your Air Fryer, and cook for 10 minutes at 300° F.
3. When the timer reaches 0, then press the cancel button
4. Arrange on a tray and serve as an appetizer.
Enjoy!

Cheese Sticks

Ready in about 40 min | Servings 16 | Normal

Ingredients:

- 2 eggs, whisked
- Salt and black pepper to the taste
- 8 mozzarella cheese strings, cut into halves
- 1 cup of parmesan, grated
- 1 tablespoon of Italian seasoning
- Cooking spray
- 1 garlic clove, minced

Directions:

1. Grab a package of mozzarella string cheese and cut each of the sticks in half. Place them into a baggie and freeze. Arrange the cheese in the tray of your Air Fryer and roast for 9 minutes at 390° F.

2. Freeze them, so the outside has a chance to get crispy before the cheese melts too much.

3. Air fry! All you do is pre-heat, place the mozzarella stick into the Air Fryer, and "fry" for 5 minutes.

4. Serve like as an appetizer.

Enjoy!

Sweet Bacon Snack

Ready in about 40 min | Servings 16 | Normal

Ingredients:

- ½ teaspoon of cinnamon powder
- 16 bacon slices
- 1 tablespoon of avocado oil
- 3 ounces of dark chocolate
- 1 teaspoon of maple extract

Directions:

1. Arrange bacon slices in the Air Fryer basket, sprinkle the cinnamon mixture over them, and prepare them for 30 minutes at 300° F.
2. Heat a pot over medium heat with the oil, add the chocolate and stir until it melts.
3. Add extract of the syrup, mix, take off the heat, and allow to cool down a little.
4. Take the bacon strips out of the oven, leave them to cool down, dip each in a mixture of chocolate, put them on parchment paper, and let them cool down.
5. Serve as a snack, like ice.
Enjoy!

Pork Burger Cutlets

Ready in about 35 min | Servings 2 | Normal

Ingredients:

- ½ lb. of pork (Make sure that you mince the pork fine)
- ½ cup of breadcrumbs
- A pinch of salt to taste
- ¼ teaspoon of ginger finely chopped
- 1 green chili finely chopped
- 1 teaspoon of lemon juice
- 1 tablespoon. of fresh coriander leaves. Chop them finely
- ¼ teaspoon of red chili powder
- ½ cup of boiled peas
- ¼ teaspoon of cumin powder
- ¼ teaspoon of dried mango powder

Directions:

1. Take a pot and add all the masalas, onions, green chilies, peas, cilantro leaves, lemon juice, ginger, and 1-2 tbsp into the breadcrumbs.
2. Add the sliced pork. I combine all the ingredients. Mold the mixture into Cutlets Round. Kindly press them back. Now scrupulously roll them out.
3. Preheat the Air Fryer for 5 minutes, at 250° F. Open the Fryer's box and place the Cutlets in the pan. Near gently.
4. Hold the fryer at about 10 to 12 minutes, at 150° F. Turn the Cutlets over in between the cooking process to get a standard dish. Serve sweet chutney with basil.

Lamb fries

Ready in about 40 min | Servings 2 | Normal

Ingredients:

- 1 lb. of boneless lamb cut into fingers
- 2 cup of dry breadcrumbs
- 2 teaspoon of oregano
- 2 teaspoon of red chili flakes
- For the Marinade:
- 1 ½ tbsp. of ginger-garlic paste
- 4 tablespoon of lemon juice
- 2 teaspoon of salt
- 1 teaspoon of pepper powder
- 1 teaspoon of red chili powder
- 6 tablespoon of cornflour
- 4 eggs

Directions:

1. Mix all the marinade ingredients, put the lamb's fingers inside, and let it rest overnight. Mix well the breadcrumbs, oregano, and red chili flakes, then placing the marinated fingers on the mixture.

2. Cover with plastic wrap and keep before just before starting food—prefire up the Air Fryer for 5 minutes at 160° F.

3. Place your fingers in and close the fry box. Let them cook for another 15 minutes at the same time, or so. Flip well the fingers until they are fried equally.

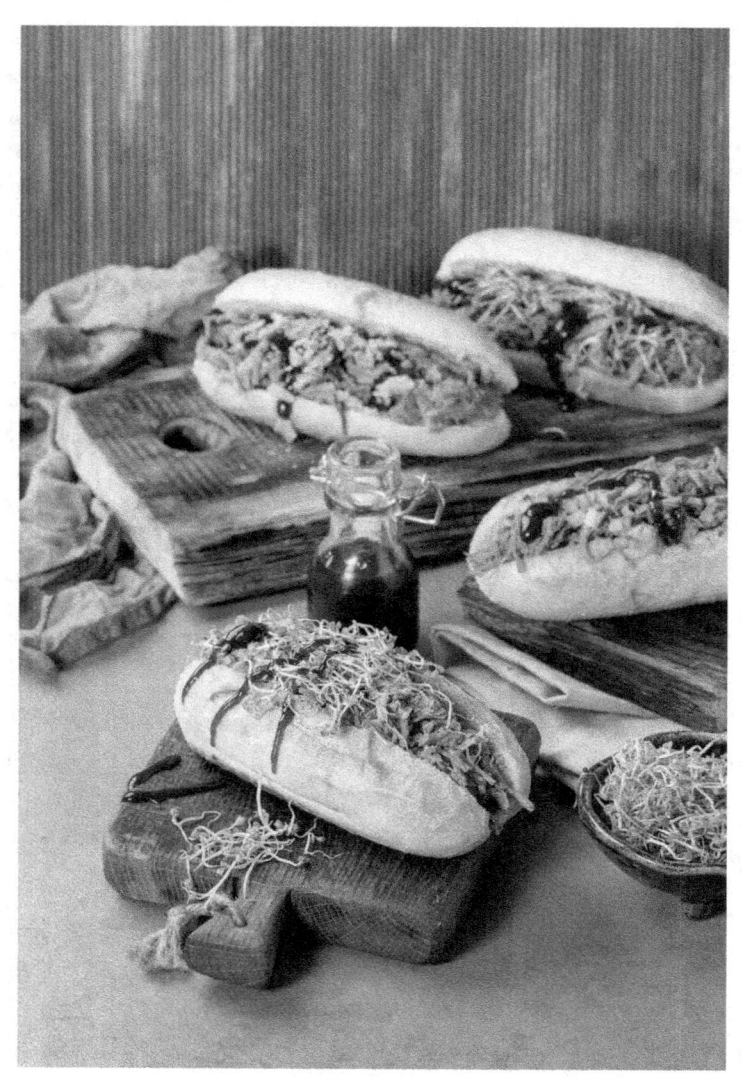

Barbecue Pork Club Sandwich

Ready in about 25 min | Servings 2 | Normal

Ingredients:

- 2 slices of white bread
- 1 tablespoon of softened butter
- ½ lb. of cut pork (Get the meat cut into cubes)
- 1 small capsicum

For Barbeque Sauce:

- ¼ tablespoon of Worcestershire sauce
- ½ teaspoon of olive oil
- ½ flake of garlic crushed
- ¼ cup of chopped onion
- ¼ teaspoon of mustard powder
- ½ tablespoon of sugar
- ¼ tablespoon of red chili sauce
- 1 tablespoon of tomato ketchup
- ½ cup of water.

Directions:

1. Take the bread slices and cut the rims. Still cut horizontally on the strips. Heat the sauce ingredients and wait before the sauce thickens. Now apply the pork to the sauce and whisk before the flavors are acquired.

2. Whisk the capsicum and scrape off the flesh. The capsicum is sliced into strips. Mix the ingredients, and add them to the slices of bread.

3. Preheat the Air Fryer about 300° F for 5 minutes. Open the Fryer's basket and put the cooked sandwiches in it, ensuring that no two sandwiches meet each other. Hold the fryer at about 15 minutes now at 250° F

4. Switch the sandwiches to cook both slices in between the cooking process. Serve the strawberry ketchup or mint chutney sandwiches.

Pork Burger Cutlets

Ready in about 30 min | Servings 2 | Normal

Ingredients:

- ½ lb. of pork (Make sure that you mince the pork fine)
- ½ cup of breadcrumbs
- A pinch of salt to taste
- ¼ teaspoon of ginger finely chopped
- 1 green chili finely chopped
- 1 teaspoon of lemon juice
- 1 tablespoon of fresh coriander leaves. Chop them finely
- ¼ teaspoon of red chili powder
- ½ cup of boiled peas
- ¼ teaspoon of cumin powder
- ¼ teaspoon of dried mango powder

Directions:

1. Take a pot and add all the masalas, onions, green chilies, peas, cilantro leaves, lemon juice, ginger, and 1-2 tablespoon into it. Breadcrumbs, crumbs. Then add the sliced pork.

2. Combine all the ingredients. Mold the mixture into Cutlets Round. Kindly press them back. Now scrupulously roll them out.

3. Preheat the Air Fryer for 5 minutes, at 250° F. Open the Fryer's box and place the Cutlets in the pan. Hold the fryer at about 10 to 12 minutes, at 150°F. Turn the Cutlets over in between the cooking process to get a classic dish. Serve nice with mint chutney.

Tasty Kale and Celery Crackers

Ready in about 30 min | Servings 6 | Normal

Ingredients:

- 2 cups of flaxseed, ground
- 2 cups of flax seed, soaked overnight and drained
- 4 bunches of kale, chopped
- 1 bunch of basil, chopped
- ½ bunch of celery, chopped
- 4 garlic cloves, minced
- 1/3 cup of olive oil

Directions:

1. Mix the ground flaxseed with the celery, kale, basil, and garlic in your food processor and mix well.
2. Add the oil and soaked flaxseed, then mix again, scatter in the pan of your Air Fryer, break into medium crackers and cook for 20 minutes at 380° F.
3. When the timer reaches 0, then press the cancel button
4. Serve as an appetizer and break into cups.

Enjoy!

Tuna Cakes

Ready in about 20 min | Servings 12 | Normal

Ingredients:

- 15 ounces of canned tuna, drain and flaked
- 3 eggs
- ½ teaspoon of dill, dried
- 1 teaspoon of parsley, dried
- ½ cup of red onion, chopped
- 1 teaspoon of garlic powder
- Salt and black pepper to the taste
- Cooking spray

Directions:

1. Mix the tuna with salt, pepper, dill, parsley, onion, garlic powder, and eggs in a cup, whisk well, and make medium cakes out of the mixture.
2. Place the tuna cakes in the basket of your Air Fryer, spray them with the cooking oil and cook for 10 minutes at 350° F and turn them halfway.
3. When the timer reaches 0, then press the cancel button
4. Place them on a tray and act as an appetizer.

Enjoy!

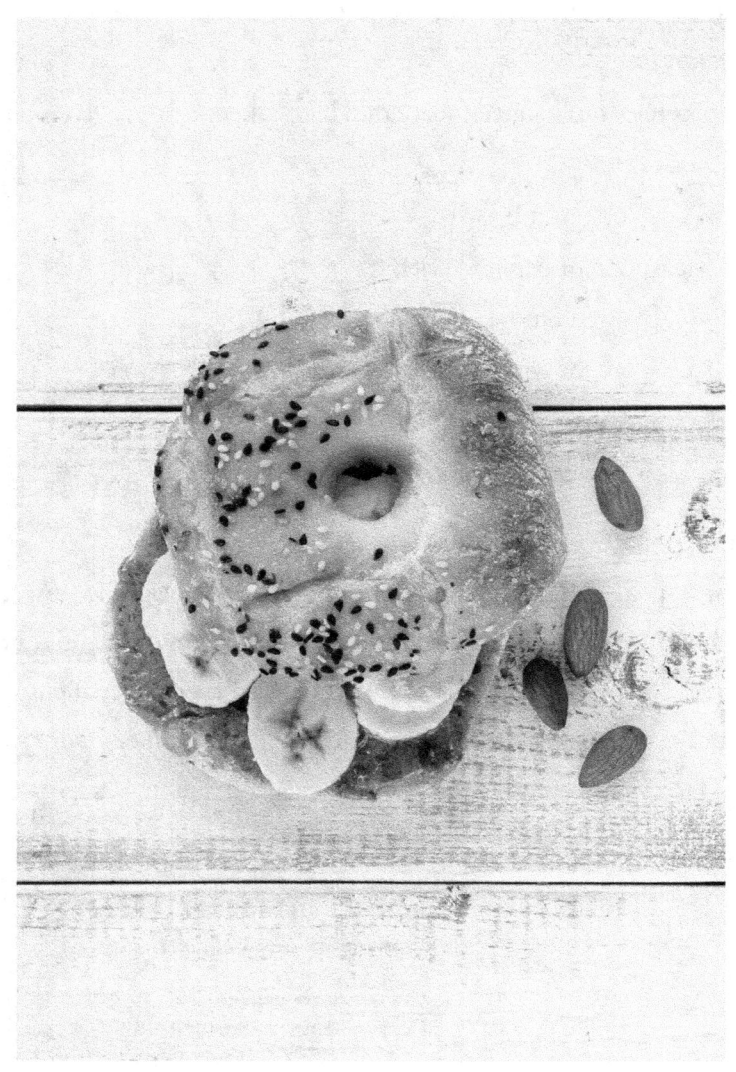

Toasted Seasoned Nuts

Ready in about 55 min | Servings 3 | Normal

Ingredients:

- ¼ teaspoon of garlic cloves, ground
- ½ pound of cashews
- 4 tablespoons of sugar
- 8 ounces of pecan halves
- 1 egg white, whisked
- 1 teaspoon of salt
- ½ teaspoon of cinnamon
- ¼ teaspoon of mixed spice
- ¼ teaspoon of cayenne pepper
- 1 cup of almonds

Directions:

1. Mix the sugar, garlic, mixed spice, pepper, salt, cinnamon, and egg in a bowl.
2. Select bake mode the set the temperature to heat your Air Fryer to 300°F.
3. Put the cashews, almonds, and pecan into the egg mixture and toss.
4. Coat the fryer basket with oil using a brush and pour half the nut mixture on it. Toast for 25 minutes until crunchy, stirring the nuts at intervals. Do the same with the second batch of nuts.
5. Store in a sealed jar if not eaten immediately.

Nacho Coated Prawns

Ready in about 30 min | Servings 3-4 | Normal

Ingredients:

- 9 ounces of nacho chips
- 1 egg, whisked
- 18 medium-sized prawns

Directions:

1. Remove the shell and veins from the prawns, wash thoroughly, and wipe dry.
2. Grind the chips in a bowl until pieces areas that of breadcrumbs.
3. Dip each prawn into the egg and then coat with the chip crumbs.
4. Select bake mode the set the temperature to heat the Air Fryer to 356° F.
5. Put the prawns into the Air Fryer and cook for 8 minutes. Serve with salsa or sour cream.

Cheesy Mustard and Ham Rounds

Ready in about 45 min | Servings 6 | Normal

Ingredients:

- 2 cups of Gruyere cheese, grated
- 6 slices of ham
- 1 tablespoon of mustard
- 1 sheet of pre-rolled puff pastry

Directions:

1. Cover your workbench with flour and put the pastry on it.

2. Add the ham, mustard, and cheese evenly on the pastry and roll up beginning from the shorter edge.

3. Cover with cling film and place in the freezer until firm for 30 minutes. Remove, and slice into 1cm thick small circles.

4. Select bake mode the set the temperature to heat your Air Fryer to 370°F and cook the rounds in it until golden brown for 10 minutes.

Grilled Cheese Delight

Ready in about 15 min | Servings 2 | Normal

Ingredients:

- 4 slices of white bread
- ¼ cup of butter, melted
- ½ cup of sharp cheddar cheese

Directions:

1. Select bake mode the set the temperature to preheat the Air Fryer to 360°F. Place the butter and cheese in two separate bowls.

2. Brush the butter on both sides of the bread. Place the cheese on 2 of the 4 bread pieces.

3. Put together the grilled cheese and add to the Air Fryer cooking basket.

4. Cook until the cheese has melted and is golden brown or for 5 to 7 minutes.

5. Serves and Enjoy

Roti Prata Mini Sausage Rolls

Ready in about 20 min | Servings 4 | Normal

Ingredients:

- 1 packet of Roti Prata
- 10 mini beef sausage

Directions:

1. Slice the Prata into triangles. Roll each sausage in a prata triangle until all are well wrapped.

2. Select bake mode the set the temperature to heat your Air Fryer to 356°F and place the rolls in the fryer basket.

3. Bake them for 15 minutes until crispy, turning the rolls halfway through.

4. Serve and Enjoy

Filo Covered Apple Pie

Ready in about 28 min | Servings 8 | Normal

Ingredients:

- 3 large apples, finely chopped
- 6 teaspoons of sugar
- 6 ounces of melted butter
- 10 sheets of filo pastry
- 2 teaspoons of cinnamon
- 2 teaspoons of flour
- ½ teaspoon of cloves, ground
- ½ teaspoon of nutmeg, ground
- 3 teaspoons of lemon juice

Directions:

1. Mix the apples, flour, lemon juice, cloves, cinnamon, nutmeg, and sugar together in a bowl.

2. Place the filo pastry on a clean surface, unroll and brush gently with butter.

3. Spoon some apple filling and place on the filo sheets about 2" away from the base. Fold the base of the sheet and then a third of the length over the filling. Roll-up the entire filling with the filo sheet to form a triangle shape, brushing the edges with butter.

4. Coat all sides of the filo triangles with the melted butter and sprinkle some sugar on top.

5. Select bake mode the set the temperature to heat your Air Fryer to 320° F and cook the apple pies in batches for 8 minutes, depending on the size. Remove when they appear light brown and crisp.

Serve while warm.

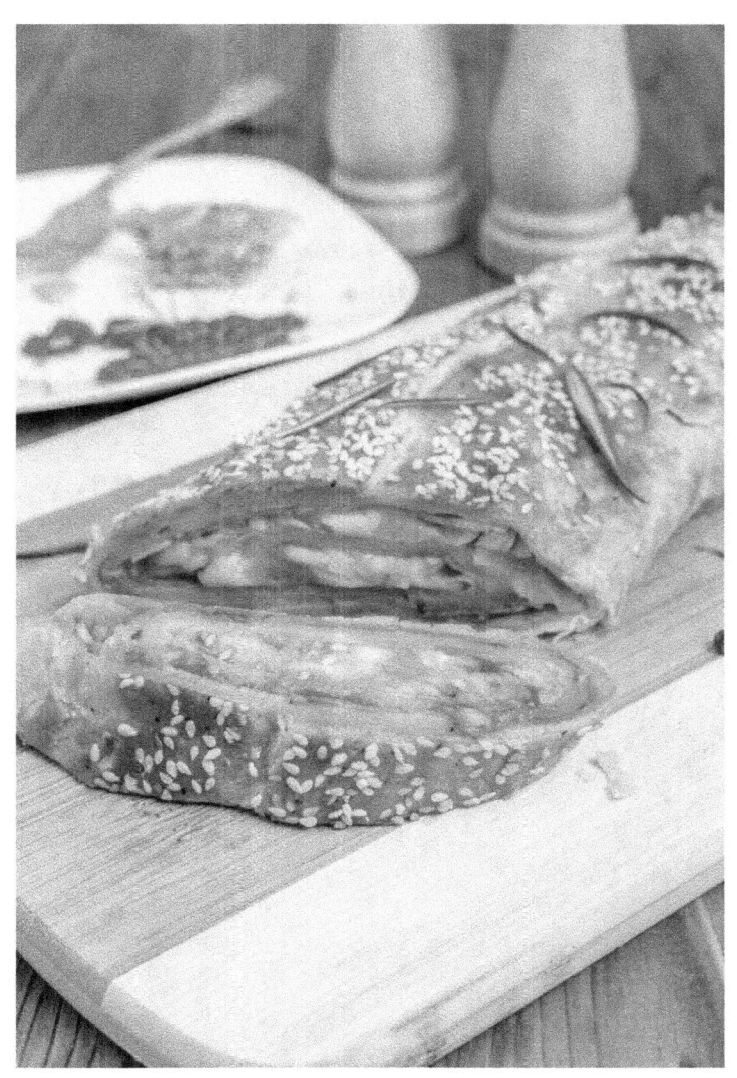

Puff Pastry Banana Rolls

Ready in about 20 min | Servings 3 | Normal

Ingredients:
- 2 puff pastry sheets
- medium-sized bananas, peeled

Directions:

1. Cut the pastry sheets into thin strips—twine two strips to form a cord. Make as many cords as needed.

2. Wind the bananas with the cords until the entire banana is covered with the pastry.

3. Select bake mode the set the temperature to heat your Air Fryer to 356°F and cook the wrapped bananas for about 10 minutes until golden.

4. Serves

Crunchy Sweet Potato Sticks

Ready in about 15 min | Servings 1 | Normal

Ingredients:

- 1 medium-sized sweet potato
- Salt to taste
- 1 teaspoon of coconut oil
- 1 tablespoon of aioli

Directions:

1. Select bake mode the set the temperature to heat your Air Fryer to 200°F.
2. Cut the sweet potato into sticks and toss in the coconut oil.
3. Place the potato sticks into the cooking basket and fry for 10 minutes until they turn crisp.
4. Add the salt and serve with aioli.

Spring Rolls

Ready in about 22 min | Servings 20 | Normal

Ingredients:

- 3 teaspoon of olive oil
- 1 small sized onion, diced
- 2 ounces of Asian noodles
- 1 packet of spring roll wrappers
- 3 cloves of garlic, crushed
- 8 ounces of mixed vegetables
- 1 teaspoon of soy sauce
- 7 ounces of mince
- 6 teaspoons of water

Directions:

1. Put the noodles in hot water, allowing it to soak until soft; drain it, then cut into shorter length.

2. Heat the oil in a skillet, then add the onion, mixed vegetables, mince, and garlic. Cook the mixture until mince is soft, then add soy sauce.

3. Remove from heat and mix with the noodles. Allow standing until the noodles absorb the juices.

4. Place the spring roll wrapper, one after the other, and add the noodle mixture diagonally across. Fold the pointed edge close to the filling over it, then fold the 2 side points together. Brush the last point with water, then roll over the spring roll to seal it.

5. Select bake mode the set the temperature to heat the Air Fryer to 356°F.

6. Coat each roll with oil using a pastry brush in a single layer in Air Fryer to cook for 8 minutes. Cook in batches until all rolls are cooked.

Syrupy Buttered Figs with Mascarpone

Ready in about 15 min | Servings 4 | Normal

Ingredients:

- 2 tablespoons of butter
- 5.2 ounces of mascarpone
- 1 teaspoon of rose water
- 8 figs
- 1½ ounces of maple syrup toasted almonds

Directions:

1. Select bake mode the set the temperature to preheat the Air Fryer to 350° F.
2. Cut the top of the figs vertically and horizontally to form a cross and squeeze the bottom lightly to open.
3. Put a small lump of butter into each fig and place in a dish. Drizzle the maple syrup over the figs.
4. Place the dish into the Air Fryer basket and cook for 5 minutes until soft.
5. Pour the rosewater into the mascarpone and stir. Place a spoonful in each serving and sprinkle the almond on top.

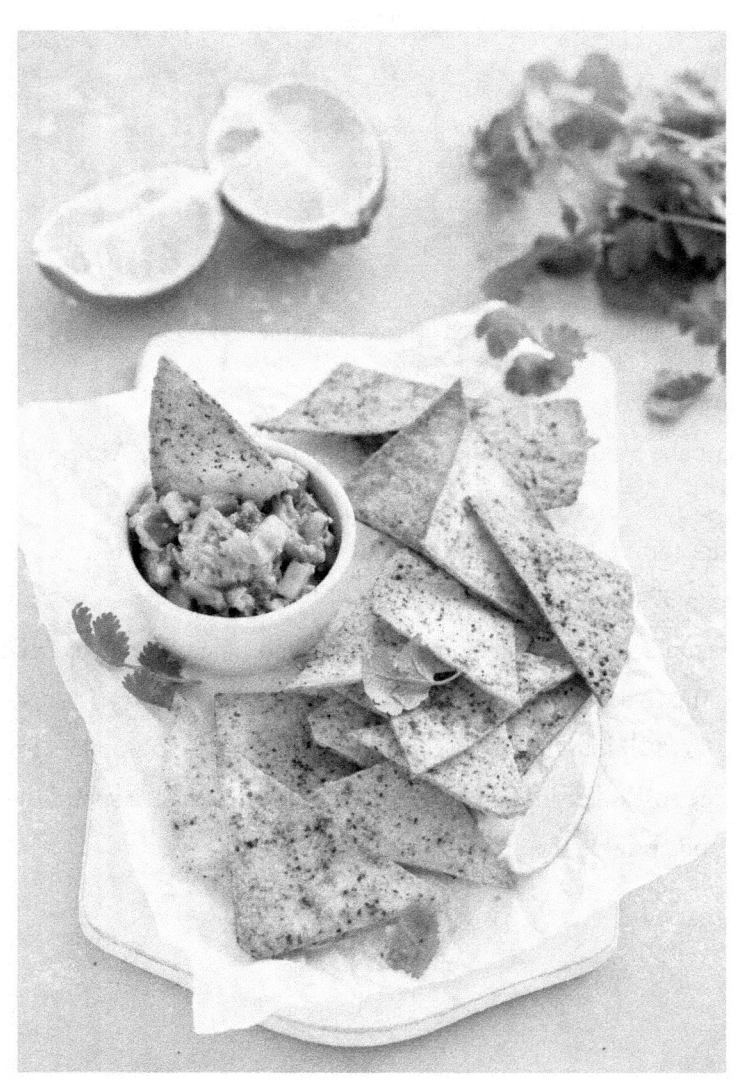

Corn Tortilla Chips

Ready in about 7 min | Servings 3 | Normal

Ingredients:

- 6 teaspoons of vegetable oil
- 8 Corn Tortillas
- Salt to the taste

Directions:

1. Select bake mode the set the temperature to heat the Air Fryer to 390°F.
2. Cut out shapes from the tortillas using a knife. Coat the tortillas with oil using a pastry brush.
3. Put half the tortilla into the fryer basket and cook for 3 minutes. Do the same with the second batch until all the chips are ready.
4. Add the salt and serve hot with a sauce.

Air Fried Banana Chips

Ready in about 30 min | Servings 4 | Normal

Ingredients:

- 3 medium-sized bananas, peeled
- 1 teaspoon of vegetable oil
- ½ teaspoon of Chaat masala seasoning
- ½ teaspoon of Turmeric powder
- 1 teaspoon of salt

Directions:

1. Add about 1½ cups of water to the turmeric powder and a little salt. Slice the bananas into the turmeric mixture to prevent it from getting black by giving it a yellow color. Soak the bananas for 10 minutes and then drain off and dry.

2. Select bake mode the set the temperature to heat your Air Fryer to 356° F for 5 minutes

3. Add the oil to the chips and toss lightly—Fry for 15 minutes in the Air Fryer. Remove from the fryer and add the salt and seasoning. Serve immediately or preserve in an airtight container.

Rosemary Chips

Ready in about 1hr 10 min | Servings 4 | Normal

Ingredients:

- 2 teaspoons of finely chopped rosemary
- 4 russet potatoes
- 3 teaspoons of olive oil
- ¼ teaspoon of salt

Directions:

1. Peel potatoes and slice them into thin chips. Soak them in water for 30 minutes, drain and then pat dry with a paper towel.

2. Select bake mode the set the temperature to heat your Air Fryer to about 330° F.

3. Pour the olive oil into the potato chips and toss until all the potatoes are coated.

4. Put the potatoes into the fryer basket and air fry for 30 minutes until golden and crisp. Shake often during cooking to ensure the potatoes are evenly cooked.

4. Remove from fryer, add the rosemary and salt and toss to mix.

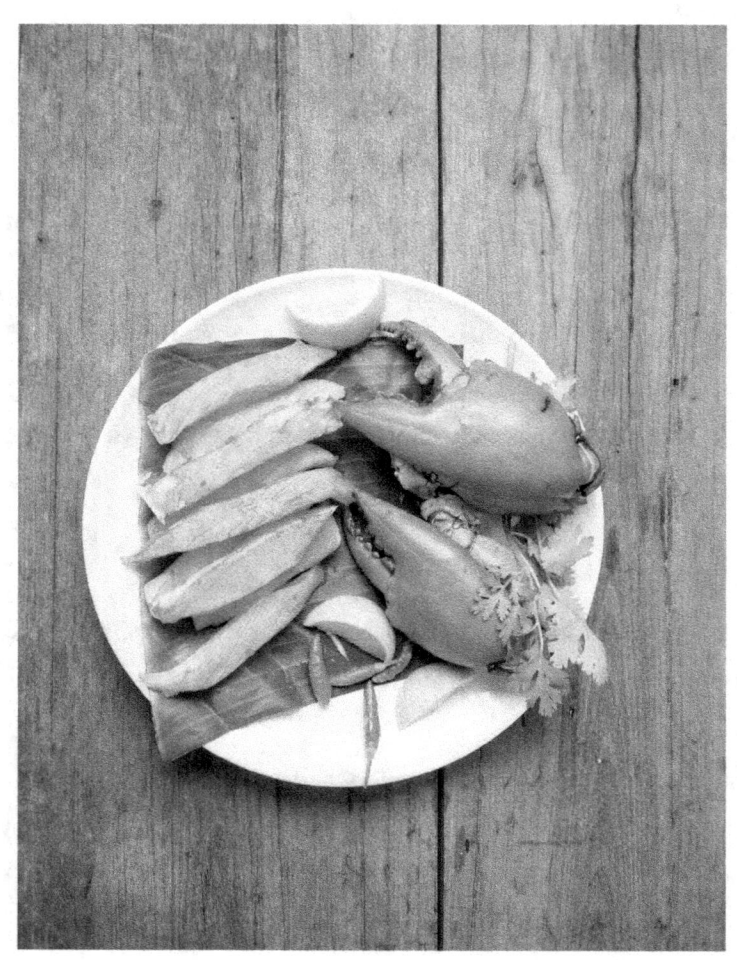

Air Fried Crab Sticks

Ready in about 17 min | Servings 1-2 | Normal

Ingredients:

- 1 packet crabsticks, break length-wise and cut into even small pieces
- 2 teaspoon oil
- Cajun or curry seasoning powder (optional)

Directions:

1. Select bake mode the set the temperature to preheat Air Fryer at 325° F for 5 minutes. Place cut and even crab sticks in a bowl and drizzle oil over, tossing well to combine.

2. Air fry until golden brown for 12 minutes. Every few minutes, check to ensure they are cooking evenly.

3. Sprinkle with seasoning if desired.

Bread Rolls with Crisp Potato Stuffing

Ready in about 35 min | Servings 8 | Normal

Ingredients:

- 8 slice bread, white part only
- 5 large potatoes
- 2green chilies, seeded and finely chopped
- 1 small coriander bunch, finely chopped
- 1/2 teaspoon of turmeric
- 2 small onions, finely chopped
- 1/2 teaspoon of mustard seeds
- 2 tablespoons of oil
- 2 sprigs curry leaf
- Salt to the taste

Directions

1. Add the potato, a spoon of salt, and water to a pot. Boil, peel, and mash the potatoes thoroughly.
2. Heat a teaspoon of oil and mustard seeds in a pan. Once they sputter, add the onions and Fry until translucent and the curry leaves and add turmeric. Fry and then add the mashed potatoes and salt. Mix well and let it cool.
3. Using your palms, shape the mixture into 8 oval shapes and set aside.
4. Now, trim off the sides of the bread and wet it totally with water. Remove excess water by pressing with your palm.
5. Keeping the wet bread in your palm, place the potato, and roll the bread in a spindle shape. Afterward, seal the edges and ensure that the potato filling is wholly inside the bread.

6. Make all the rolls and brush with oil. Keep aside. Preheat the Air Fryer at 400° F for 8 minutes and brush the basket with some oil before placing the ready rolls.

7. Cook 12-13 minutes until golden crisp. Enjoy with tomato ketchup along with masala chai!

Feta and Onion Bell Pepper Rolls

Ready in about 35 min | Servings 8 | Normal

Ingredients:

- 4 medium-sized bell red and yellow peppers
- 2 tablespoons of finely chopped basil
- 1 green onion, thinly sliced
- 3½ ounces of feta cheese, grated
- 8 toothpicks or tapas forks

Directions:

1. Heat your Air Fryer to 392° F.
2. Place the peppers into the fryer basket and Air Fry for 10 minutes until they are charred to an extent.
3. Mix the feta cheese, basil, and green onions in a bowl and set aside.
4. Bring out the bell peppers and cut them vertically into halves, remove skin and the seeds.
5. Put the feta-onion mixture into each pepper and roll up beginning from the thinner end. Fasten the rolls with a toothpick of a tapas fork and serve.

Spicy Coconut Coated Shrimp

Ready in about 24 min | Servings 4 | Normal

Ingredients:

- 4 ounces of grated coconut
- 16 ounces of large-sized shrimps, peeled, deveined
- 4 ounces of flour
- 2 egg whites, whisked
- 8 tablespoons of breadcrumbs
- ½ teaspoon of salt Zest of 1 small lemon
- Sweet chili sauce
- ½ teaspoon of ground black pepper
- Oil spray

Directions:

1. Mix the breadcrumbs with the zest, pepper, coconut, and salt in a dish and set aside. Season the flour with pepper and salt in a separate dish. Put the eggs in another dish.
2. Heat your Air Fryer to 400° F.
3. Put each shrimp into the flour, then dip into the whisked eggs, and lastly, coat evenly with the breadcrumb mixture.
4. Place the dredged shrimps on a plate and coat with oil using an oil spray.
5. Divide the shrimps into two batches and place the first into the Air Fryer. Cook for 6 minutes until firm. Do the same with the second batch. Turn down the temperature to 340° F and add the first batch to the Air Fryer second. Air Fry for 2 more minutes.
6. Best served with sweet chili sauce.

Crispy French Fries

Ready in about 1hr min | Servings 8 | Normal

Ingredients:

- 6 teaspoons of vegetable oil
- 6 medium-sized Irish potatoes

Directions

1. Peel potatoes and slice them into 3" long strips. Soak them in water for 30 minutes, drain, and then dry with a paper towel.
2. Select bake mode the set the temperature to heat your Air Fryer to about 360° F.
3. Pour the oil into the potato strips and toss until thoroughly mixed.
4. Put the potatoes in the Fryer basket and cook until golden for 30 minutes, shaking at 10 minutes intervals.

Bacon-Wrapped Shrimp

Ready in about 35 min | Servings 4 | Normal

Ingredients:

- 16 pieces (1¼ pounds) of tiger shrimp, peeled and deveined
- 16 slices (1-pound) of bacon, thinly sliced

Directions:

1. Wrap a slice of bacon around the shrimp completely. Refrigerate the wrapped shrimp for 20 minutes.
2. Select bake mode the set the temperature to preheat the Air Fryer to 390° F. Take the shrimp out from the refrigerator and place it in the cooking basket.
3. Cool for 5 to 7 minutes. Drain on a paper towel and serve.

Sage and Onion Stuffing Balls Air-Fryer

Ready in about 18 min | Servings 9 | Normal

Ingredients:

- 3.5 oz of sausage meat
- ½ small onion, peeled and diced
- 1 teaspoon of sage
- ½ teaspoon of garlic puree
- 3 tablespoons of breadcrumbs
- Salt and pepper to the taste

Directions:

1. Combine all ingredients in a bowl and mix well.
2. Form mixture into medium-sized balls and place in the Air Fryer
3. Cook at 350° F for 15 minutes. Serve and enjoy!

Chenjehn

Ready in about 55 min | Servings 2 | Normal

Ingredients:

- 2 lb. of mutton chopped
- 3 onions chopped
- 5 green chilies-roughly chopped
- 1 ½ tablespoons of ginger paste
- 1 teaspoon of garlic paste
- 1 ½ teaspoon of salt
- 3 teaspoon of lemon juice
- 2 teaspoon of garam masala
- 4 tablespoons of chopped coriander
- 3 tablespoons of cream
- 2 tablespoons of coriander powder
- 4 tablespoons of fresh mint (chopped)
- 3 t tablespoons of chopped capsicum
- 2 tablespoons of peanut flour
- 3 eggs

Directions:

1. In a tub, mix dry ingredients. Turn the mixture into a thick paste, and cover the mixture with the cubes of the mutton.

2. Place the eggs in a cup, then apply salt. Dip the cubes into the mixture of the eggs and coat them with seeds and leave them in the fridge for an hour. At 290° F, preheat the Air Fryer for around 5 minutes. Place the kebabs in the basket and make them cook at the same temperature for another 25 minutes. To get a standard cook to switch the kebabs over during the cooking process. Serve with mint chutney kebabs.

Juicy Kebab

Ready in about 30 min | Servings 2 | Normal

Ingredients:

- 2 lb. of chicken breasts cubed
- 3 onions chopped
- 5 green chilies-roughly chopped
- 1 ½ tablespoons of ginger paste
- 1 ½ teaspoon of garlic paste
- 1 ½ teaspoon of salt
- 3 teaspoon of lemon juice
- 2 teaspoon of garam masala
- 4 tablespoons of chopped coriander
- 3 t tablespoons of cream
- 2 tablespoons of coriander powder
- 4 tablespoons. of fresh mint (chopped)
- 3 tablespoons of chopped capsicum
- 2 tablespoons of peanut flour
- 3 eggs

Directions:

1. In a tub, mix dry ingredients. Turn the mixture into a thick paste, and cover the mixture with the chicken cubes.

2. Place the eggs in a cup, then apply salt. Dip the cubes into the mix of the eggs and coat them with sesame seeds and leave them in the fridge for an hour.

3. At 290° F, Preheat the Air Fryer for around 5 minutes. Place the kebabs in the basket and make them cook at the same temperature for another 25 minutes. To get a standard cook to switch the kebabs over during the cooking process. Serve with mint chutney kebabs.

Banana Rolls

Ready about in: 20 min| Serves 3|Easy

Ingredients

- 3 ripe bananas.
- Agar-agar prepared in water
- Wheat flour.
- 1 teaspoon baking soda
- 1 teaspoon cinnamon
- 1 teaspoon ginger
- 1/2 teaspoon cloves
- 1/4 teaspoon salt
- 3 large eggs
- 1 cup granulated sugar
- 6 ounces cream cheese, softened
- 5 Tablespoons butter
- 3 cups powdered sugar
- 1 teaspoon vanilla

Directions:

Heat your Air Fryer to 375° F,

Stir together flour, baking powder, baking soda, cinnamon, ginger, cloves and salt in small bowl

Beat eggs and granulated sugar in large mixer bowl until thick

Stir in flour mixture

Spread evenly into prepared pan

Bake for 10 to 12 minutes or until the top of cake springs back when touched cool on wire rack

While it cools make the frosting: beat cream cheese, butter, and vanilla extract until smooth,

spread frosting over cake

Re-roll the cake then wrap in plastic wrap and freeze

remove from the freezer let sit for 10 minutes.

Serve and Enjoy!

Milanese Of Eggplant

Ready about in: 15 min| Serve 2|Easy

Ingredients

- Eggplants
- Chickpea flour
- Traditional flour
- Water
- Breadcrumbs
- Oregano
- Cumin
- Garlic Powder
- Salt

Directions:

Mix the cornmeal and chickpea with the water in a bowl.

Add cumin, oregano, garlic powder, salt, and mix. In an other container place the breadcrumbs.

Peel and cut along the eggplant and set aside. Pass the eggplant one by one through the flour mixture, and then through the breadcrumbs.

Place in the Air Fryer and fry for 6 minutes at 390° F.

Serve and Enjoy!

Uruguayan Fried Cakes

Ready about in: 20 min|Serves 2|Normal

Ingredients

- 2 cups of wheat flour.
- 1 ½ teaspoon of baking powder.
- ½ tablespoon of salt.
- 4 tablespoons of oil.
- 1 cup of soy milk
- Agar-agar diluted in water
- Lemon zest.
- Sugar.

Directions:

1.2 separate preparation s are made. On the one hand, the agar-agar, oil and ½ cup of milk are mixed.

2.Mix up to foam. On the other hand, the remaining ingredients are mixed.

3.Then mix the 2 mixtures and knead very well, until they stick to the mold.

4.If necessary, more milk is added. Rest for 10 minutes.

Make small balls, then stretch.

5.Make a cross cut and put in the Air Fryer for 8 - 12 minutes at 380° F.

6.They bathe with sugar when re moving them from the Fryer.

Serve and Enjoy!

Delicious Malanga

Ready about in: 15 min|Serves 2|Normal

Ingredients

- 3 medium malangas
- 200g vegan cream cheese
- 2 Parsley
- 5 cloves of garlic
- Pepper
- Salt
- Chives

Directions:

1. Peel and grate the raw malanga.

2. Knead with all the ingredients and bring to the Air Fryer for 6 - 10 minutes at 380° F.

3. When the timer reaches 0, then press the cancel button

Serve and Enjoy!

Artichoke Croquettes

Ready about in: 15 min| Serves 2|Normal

Ingredients

- 6 artichoke backgrounds
- ½ kg of soy meat
- 2 slices of bread without skin
- Minced garlic
- 1 cup of flour
- Salt pepper
- 1cdta of sugar
- Lemon juice to taste.

Directions:

1. Hydrate the soy meat for 10 minutes, and then drain well.
2. Salt pepper the meat. Make a mixture of egg, garlic, salt, and pepper.
3. Add bread, lemon juice, sugar and knead well. Mix the artichokes in the previous preparation and then pass them through beaten egg and flour.
4. Place them in the Air Fryer for a period of 6 - 10 minutes at 360°

Serve and Enjoy!

Caramelized Bananas

Ready about in: 45 min| Serves 2|Normal

Ingredients

- Ripe bananas.
- 2 tablespoons Brown sugar or brown paper.
- Cinnamon powder.
- water

Directions:

1. Peel the bananas and cut them into pieces.

2. Place them in a small pot with a little oil and sprinkle with the ingredient.

3. Fry in Air Fryer for 35 minutes at 360° F.

Serve and Enjoy!

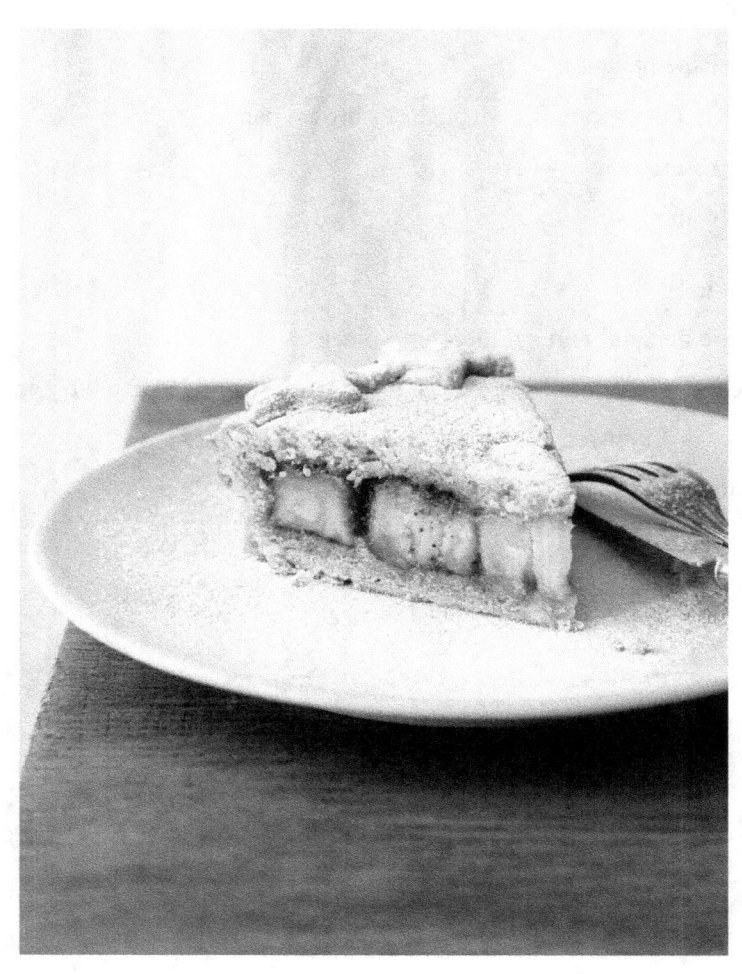

Banana Pie

Ready about in: 1 hr and 20 min| Serves 3|Easy

Ingredients

- 3 Ripe bananas
- 1/2 cup flour
- 2 eggs
- 2 tablespoons butter
- 3 cups milk
- 2/3 cup white sugar
- 1 teaspoons vanilla
- 1 baked pastry shell
- Water
- 1 teaspoon Salt

Directions:

1.In a saucepan, combine the sugar, flour, and salt. Add milk while stirring.

2.Cook over medium heat for about 3 more minutes, and then remove from the burner.

3.Stir a small quantity of the hot mixture into the beaten egg yolks, Cook for 3 more minutes; remember to keep stirring. Remove the mixture from the stove, and add butter and vanilla.

4.Slice bananas into the cooled baked pastry shell

5.Bake at 350° F for 10 to 18 minutes. Chill for an 50 minutes.

Fried Vegan Milk

Ready about in: 15 min| Serves 3|Easy

Ingredients

- 130 gr of cornstarch
- 1 liter of vegetable milk
- 70 gr of sugar
- Peel of a lemon
- Cinnamon sticks and ground
- Flour
- Vegetable margarine

Directions:

1. Mix ½ liter of vegetable milk in a pot with the lemon peel, the cinnamon stick, and the sugar.
2. Boil for a few minutes. Remove from the fire.
3. In a separate bowl: mix the rest of the vegetable milk with the cornstarch.
4. When finished mixing mix both preparation s and bring to fire for a few minutes.
5. Place the preparation in molds and rest for a few minutes. When cooling, refrigerate.
6. When solidifying the milk, overflow in flour.
7. Place in the Air Fryer at 400° F for 2 minutes. Remove and sprinkle with sugar and ground cinnamon.

Serve up.

Celery Fritters

Ready about in: 20 min| Serves 2|Easy

Ingredients

- 1/3 kg celery.
- 1/3 cup white basil.
- Agar agar diluted in water
- Salt
- 2 cups of soy flour.
- Soy oil.
- A pinch of ginger.

Directions:

1. Wash and peel the celery. Put to parboil that is a little hard, (from 15 to 20min).

2. Chop the basil finely. Whisk the egg. Stir the celery and mix with basil, agar-agar, salt, and ginger to taste. Knead well and form balls. Roll them in the soy flour.

3. Take them to the Air Fryer at 380° F, for 8 - 12 minutes.

Serve up decorated with branches of parsley or basil to taste.

Vegan Donuts

Ready about in: 25 min| Serves 2|Easy

Ingredients

- 120 g of vegetable drink
- 50 g of vegan margarine.
- 2 tablespoons of sunflower oil
- The zest of 1 lemon.
- 250 g whole wheat flour.
- 3 teaspoon fresh yeast
- ½ teaspoon of salt
- 50 g of muscovite sugar.

Directions:

1. First, melt the margarine in a small saucepan over medium heat.
2. Add the vegetable drink and the sun flower oil. Sift all the dry ingredients in a bowl.
3. Add the lemon zest and integrate with the other ingredients. Make the shape of a volcano and integrate the liquid in the center of the mixture of the dry ones little by little with a fork.
4. When it is moldable, take it out to the table, knead it and take pieces of the dough. Stretch and cut circularly. Make a hole in the center.
5. Set the Air Fryer at 15 - 20 minutes at 260° F.
6. Put the donuts Remove and glaze with dark chocolate, sugar or whatever you prefer.

Andes Cakes

Ready about in: 30 min| Serves 2|Easy

Ingredients

- Flour all use.
- 1 cup of water.
- 1 teaspoon salt.
- 100 g of shortening.
- Cold rice
- Vegetable stew

Directions:

Dough:

1. Place the dough in a bowl; place the warm water, butter, and salt.

2. Knead little, make the dough hard. Let stand for 10 minutes. After this time, stretch with a roller and cut circles.

3. Mix the cold rice and the vegetable stew to taste. Place the dough circles by teaspoons with a brush, moisten the edges and close.

4. Puncture with a stick and fry in the Air Fryer for 8 - 15 minutes at 360°F.

5. When the timer reaches 0, then press the cancel button

Serve and Enjoy!

Apple Fritters

Ready about in: 20 min| Serves 2|Easy

Ingredients

- 2 large apples
- 200g of flour
- Salt
- A ¼ liter of cider or beer
- 1 teaspoon olive oil
- Sugar

Directions:

1. First, peel the apples and remove the seeds. Cut into rings and sprinkle sugar.
2. Add the flour in a bowl and add salt, oil, and beer. Mix sprinkle the apples in the mixture and place them in the Air Fryer tray with butter paper.
3. Fry for 10 - 15 minutes at 360° F.

Add sugar and Serve up hot.

Cinammon Apples

Ready about in: 15 min| Serves 2|Easy

Ingredients

- 2 apples
- ⅔ cups cornstarch
- 1 spoon of sugar
- ⅛ teaspoon of cinnamon
- ½ cup of caramel sauce

Directions:

1. Peel and cut the apples. Mix with the cornstarch.
2. Fry in the Air Fryer for 5 minutes at 360° F.
3. When the timer reaches 0, then press the cancel button
4. Flip to be cooked on both sides.
5. Spray cinnamon and sugar when serving.

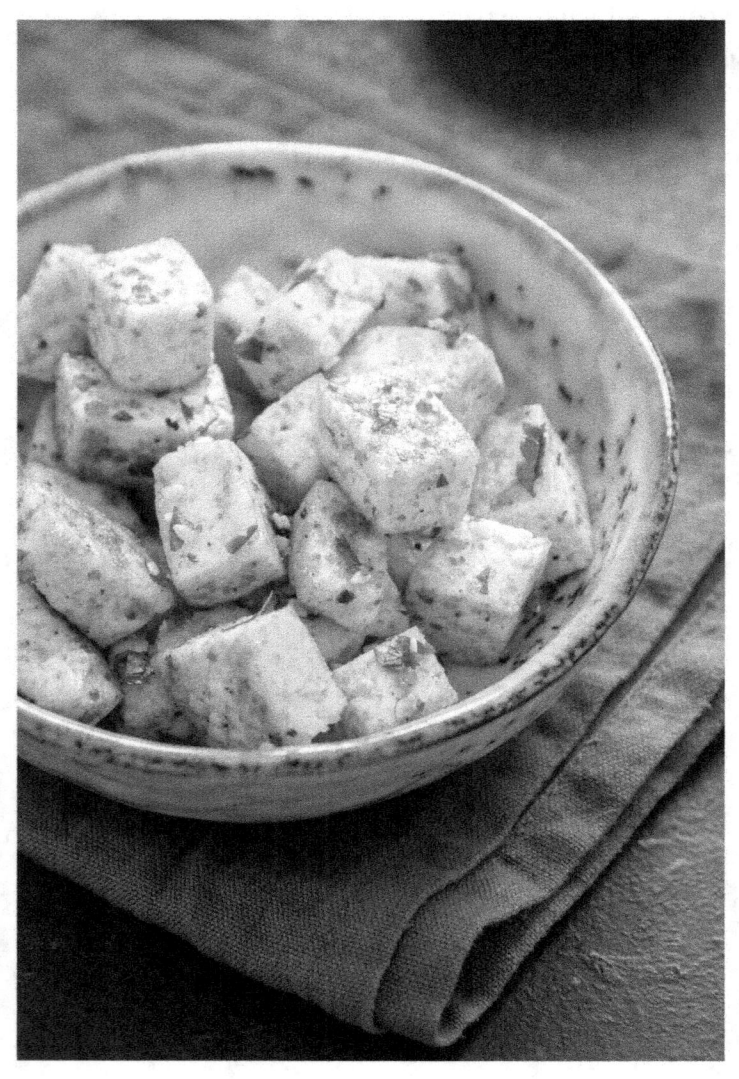

Fried Tofu

Ready about in: 15 min| Serve 2|Easy

Ingredients

- Extra Firm Tofu
- Soy sauce
- Cornstarch
- 1 pinch Chive
- 2 teaspoons vegetable oil

Directions:

1. First, remove the liquid from the tofu by pressing it. Place it on absorbent paper.
2. Cut into long squares or strips. Flour well in the cornstarch.
3. Add to the Air Fryer and fry for 8 - 10 minutes at 380° F.
4. Meanwhile, cut the chives into strips. Add tofu and continue frying. Remove and Serve up with soy sauce.

Vegan French Toast with Oregano

Ready about in: 15 min| Serves 2|Easy

Ingredients

- Cornstarch
- 250g of leavening flour
- 250g of Wheat germ
- Salt.
- Oregano.
- Pepper to taste
- 1 grated carrot
- 7 tablespoons of olive oil
- 1 glass of water

Directions:

1. Place the dry ingredients in a bowl and mix with the wet ingredients.

2. Add the grated carrot and mix. Place a little oil in the Air Fryer tray to avoid sticking.

3. Place a portion of the mixture and fry at 390° F for 5 minutes, or until golden brown.

Serve up alone or sprinkled with sugar.

Vegan Chips

Ready about in: 15 min| Serve 2|Easy

Ingredients

- 1 cucumber
- 1 clove garlic
- 1 lemon
- 350g of vegan yogurt
- 2 tablespoon of olive oil
- Salt
- Pepper to taste
- 1 sprig of parsley to decorate
- 1 yucca
- 1 sweet potato
- 1 beet
- 1 carrot

Directions:

1. Peel the cucumber and cut it in half lengthwise. Remove the seeds and grate.
2. Add a pinch of salt and remove the moisture. Process the cucumber, garlic, yogurt, lemon juice, olive oil and salt and pepper. Peel and cut the tubers into thin slices.
3. Place in the Air Fryer and fry at 380° F for 3 - 5 minutes or until crispy.
4. Sprinkle with salt and Serve up accompanied by cucumber cream.

Vegetarian Pizza

Ready about in: 55 min|Serves 4|Normal

Ingredients

- 200 gr of wheat flour
- 2 gr of yeast
- 1 pinch of salt
- 1 pinch of sugar
- Oregano to taste
- 2 olive oil
- 1 grated carrot
- Creamy vegan cheese
- Olives of your choice
- 3 slices of sliced red paprika
- Spices to taste
- Grated ginger
- 1 pinch of grated vegan cheese

Directions:

1.In a bowl, add the flour together with the yeast, salt, sugar, oregano and oil in a bowl.

2.Add little by little the warm water. Mix until the dough is solid. Knead until it forms a bun that does not stick, let it rest for more than half an hour.

3.Paint the mold of the Air Fryer with olive oil. Place the dough stretched to taste.

4.Fry at 260° F for 10 minutes or until light. Fry for 5 more minutes until golden brown. Add the cream cheese until it melts.

5.Finally, add the carrot, olives, paprika, ginger and grated cheese.

6.Fry for 2 - 3 minutes if you want to cook the vegetables.

www.ingramcontent.com/pod-product-compliance
Lightning Source LLC
Chambersburg PA
CBHW070911080526
44589CB00013B/1261